Writing A Crime Novel

DH Smith

Earlham Books

Published 2019 by Earlham Books
Book design & cover art by Lia at Free Your Words

All Rights Reserved

ISBN: 978-1-909804-36-4

CONTENTS

INTRODUCTION

This book is for you if you are thinking of writing a crime novel. Or if you are already writing one and having trouble. I will not deal with true crime, but stick strictly to fiction.

I discuss aspects of novel writing, such as character, point of view, setting and language which apply to any novel, but I concentrate on matters that are specific to the crime novel. I will illustrate it with my own writing and my own thought processes as I worked out what I wanted to write and how to do it.

This book does not deal with publishing or marketing. They will be mentioned from time to time but the focus is on writing. Publishing and marketing concerns are for another day.

First write your book.

The crime genre is a broad spectrum and a new writer needs to consider where they may fit in. Do you want to write a police procedural, or have a private eye as your main character, or go historical and have a Victorian, Tudor or Roman sleuth? I look at the types of crime novel, so you can consider what sector is right for you.

There are a few chapters on research that you may have to do. A crime writer has to convince readers that they know what they are writing about. But here's the proviso: what may satisfy most readers, may well have the professionals groaning. You have to consider how much that matters. All writers depart from best practice but some more than others.

The Concise Oxford Dictionary defines a novel as: *a fictitious prose story of book length.* 'Book length' is a sliding value, especially in these days of the ebook. I'll say 40k+, some would wish to raise the lower boundary. But it's not a fruitful argument. Novel, novella, leave the distinction to the professors. We'll get on with writing.

A novel is a game between you and the reader. You both know it isn't true, but the writer uses their art to make it appear so. The reader will go along with you if you write well.

Almost always, in the crime novel, the crime we are dealing with is murder. But murder is not the only crime in the genre; there could be a kidnapping or a robbery which may, or may not, result in murder. But even minor crimes, such as shoplifting, can have a major effect on the perpetrator and their friends or family. And so be the propellant of a novel.

Mostly it's murder. Steel yourself for killers and killings in this how-to book. Some writers delight in blood and guts writing. It is strange, and often remarked upon, that perfectly respectable people, concerned about litter and homelessness, write such gruesome tales. This can equally be applied to the readers of the genre. You are in it together. It is akin to a scary ride at the fairground, with all the sensations of falling, but safely strapped in.

Our novel must be peopled. Without a word written, without any planning at all, we already know some of the roles. We have a victim, a perpetrator, suspects, detective, witnesses, friends and family of the victim and of the perpetrator. The categories may overlap. A witness for example may be a suspect and could be a friend of the victim. The detective is often a police officer, or could be a private eye or someone who is not a professional sleuth but solves crimes as a hobby. A weird hobby, for such weird people as Lord Peter Wimsey. The detective might be a one-off detective, thrust into crime solving because, say, a brother has been wrongly accused of a crime, and so the sister sets out to find who really did it.

Our options are wide.

My aim is to encourage you to write your crime novel. To this end, I have appended exercises at the end of most chapters. I suggest you have a go at them. They are not difficult. Their purpose is to assist your creativity. In the appendix are my attempts at the exercises. I did each one myself, to prove that they are worthwhile. Having done so, I thought, why not share my efforts. That stems from my workshop days when round the table we apprentice writers read our work in turn.

I shall begin by informing you about my writing career, to show you that my credentials are sound. As it took me some time before I turned to crime, you might regard this book as my confession, and you my confessor.

A Note

The English language does not have a word for 'he or she'. I have seen 's/he' used, which I feel is fine for occasional use but I don't want to use it throughout. So I am going to use 'they'. Some consider this incorrect, but it is coming into vogue. Here's an example of what I mean: 'A murderer will leave fingerprints at the crime scene, unless they are wearing gloves.'

DH Smith

Forest Gate, London, 2019

WRITING A CRIME NOVEL

CHAPTER 1: My Writing Life

H aving graduated in 1966 with a degree in chemical technology specialising in plastics, by the end of my course, I knew I didn't like plastics. My career had begun with a wrong turn. I did some teaching, but that was never going to work for me as I didn't want to be a teacher. And as my heart was not in it, I wasn't a good one.

My writing began with bad poetry. Fortunately, that has been lost. Thrown out more likely. Then came bad plays. Not intentionally, I just didn't know what I was doing. There were four of them, again all lost along the cliff path of time. Here's hoping they have fallen into the sea and decomposed. I have no illusions there were gems in that apprentice work.

At the time, I had the naïve belief in my genius as a writer. It's a common disease in writers but it is curable, though there are those who suffer it all their lives. My plays were sent off to various theatres, and given to friends and family to read. No one liked them. I was either a misunderstood talent, ahead of my time, or the plays were bad.

Coming to the reluctant conclusion they were not all I hoped them to be, I went on a playwriting course at the City Lit (abbreviation for City Literary College) in London. I was working at the time as an assistant gardener in a park. It was a good job for a writer as the job could be left behind when I left work. It didn't pay much, but enough to get by.

1

The City Lit course was a two hour evening class. The tutor on the course was Cathy Itzen, an American who had come through the US college system where they taught playwriting and theatre. I learned that I did have some talent, but needed to learn about the craft of playwriting. Good friends were made on the course, which is not a "by the way", as fellow students appreciate what you are trying to do and can be very supportive.

After two terms, I submitted an idea based on an event that had happened in the park where I was then working. Cathy said: fine, write it. When completed, it was a 45 minute stage play that was read in the class and went down well. I wondered what to do with it. Entitled *Albert and the Mayor's Tree*, it had about twelve characters. Great for a class, too short for theatre, way too many characters for any commercial set up. So it was changed to a radio play. And over the summer, when the course was in recess, I sent it to the BBC.

The 70s

Within a month, the quickest response I've had, they accepted the play. It was performed on radio in 1972 and well received. Throughout the 70s, I continued writing plays. There were four on radio, one on TV, lots of short plays performed in theatres along with three full length plays. I went to work with Soapbox Theatre in the London Borough of Newham as their writer in residence. There, I wrote plays for the company, directed them, and ran a play-writing course. Some of my plays were naturalistic, some in a political vein, some absurd. They taught me about the importance of character, dialogue and surprise in a story.

Skills not limited to plays.

The 80s

After three years with Soapbox Theatre, with my then partner Gill Hay, I set up a bookshop. Outside the theatre environment, I had stopped writing plays, and became involved in running the bookshop, as well as working in the vegetarian cafe that was also part of The Whole Thing, the name of our multifarious establishment. There, surrounded by books, I had a go at writing a novel, spending more than a year on it. But it was an impossible mess.

I went back to the City Lit. This time for a story-writing class. I'd missed a term, and the tutor, Carol Burns, spoke in passing about things like point of view. What on earth was that? I had missed that session, so had to read it up. On discovering what it was, my fiction had more structure. I wrote some short stories. A couple were broadcast on radio.

With growing confidence, my next project was a novel for young adults, *Rich Kids*. I'd read in a book for writers that you should send off four chapters to a publisher with a short covering letter. The novel finished, I did exactly that, sending off a letter with the chapters to four publishers. When one came back, another was sent out, until after more than a year 18 publishers had been contacted. All had turned the book down; not one of them wanted the full manuscript. And so, despondent, *Rich Kids* was stuck in a drawer.

Around nine months later, I re-read it, being far enough away from the manuscript to be objective. I thought, this is good. But how was I to get a publisher to read it? Unsolicited manuscripts go into what is disparagingly known as the slush pile. There are many poor books in the slush pile, which makes it hard for any decent ones to be noticed. The office junior might take a bundle home to half scan. Not my aim at all.

I didn't want to sink in the slush.

The 90s

There had to be a new strategy to sell the book. First of all, the title was changed; it became *Hard Cash*. Then I persuaded my then partner's 11 year old son, Tom, to review it. Best handwriting, I insisted, and paid him a fiver for his troubles. His review was photocopied and sent off with a letter about the book, but *with no chapters*. The letter was addressed to a *named* person. Not to 'Dear Editor', but to 'Dear Jane Brown' as it might be. My aim was to get 'Jane Brown' to ask me for the manuscript.

It worked. Four publishers were written to and each of them wanted the full manuscript. And one of those, Faber, accepted it. I didn't inform them they had already rejected it when it had been called *Rich Kids* and sent to 'Dear Editor'. I had not changed a word bar the title.

All of which has made me somewhat cynical about publishers.

Hard Cash was well reviewed, and was read on BBC radio by Tony Robinson, now Sir Tony. It is a crime novel, though I didn't see it as such at the time. It's about two boys who find quarter of a million pounds in an empty house and decide to spend it. In my eyes, it was a family book, as much about their families as it is about crime, and I was surprised when the Faber editor called it a crime novel.

Faber published two more of my young adult novels. *Frances Fairweather Demon Striker!* was shortlisted for the Children's Book Award. The other was *Half a Bike*, which was shortlisted for a French book prize. Walker Books published a book of mine for younger children, *The Magical World of Lucy-Anne*.

From 1998, I began visiting schools as a children's author. I was also tutor for the Writing for Children course at City University. But as for publishing, everything mailed out was being rejected. It was *The Good Wolf*, a book for ten-year-olds, that altered my mindset.

This is the first paragraph of the reply received from Hodder & Stoughton:

I found 'The Good Wolf' a thoroughly enjoyable story with great characterisation. You bring the serious issues of being different and not belonging into the story, which gives it substance. It is a well written, fluent piece with a good use of language.

I distinctly recall thinking as I read this, *I've sold it! They love it.*

Maybe they did. But not enough. The next paragraph begins:

Despite finding much to praise, I do not feel it is quite right for our list.

Looking back on the letter, 21 years later, I find it somewhat unbelievable. *Well written, great characterisation, enjoyable story...* But you don't want to publish it. What on earth are you looking for?

A badly written, boring story, with weak characters perhaps.

This wasn't the only positive rejection received for *The Good Wolf*. Other publishers told me how much they liked it. But 'it didn't fit their list' either. That unarguable phrase kept coming in the mail. The book was good, they told me, but they didn't want to publish it.

I was dejected. What could I do? The only possible thing. Publish it myself.

Self-publishing wasn't that respectable in 1998. But it was do that or pulp it. I read up self-publishing on the internet and learned it had to be done well. The finished book must be indistinguishable from mainstream books.

I hired a book designer and an illustrator, and printed 2000 copies, under my imprint Earlham Books. It was published in 1999 and won the David Thomas award for the best self-published children's book of that year. And has been popular in my school visits which I began around that time.

The Noughties

Self-publishing has worked for me. Taking control, no more waiting six months to find out 'it doesn't fit our list'. I used to think good authors would always find a mainstream publisher. I don't think that now. I know of good books that have been rejected, and the writers too discouraged to press on. That's depressing. But the self-publishing revolution puts the ball firmly in the writer's court.

My *Lucy-Anne's Changing Ways* was the only self-published book in the Book Trust's 2001 list. Their editor recognised it as such and phoned me up to congratulate me. I was chuffed, but at the same time miffed, as mainstream publishers weren't interested in my books.

It's hard not to desire a pat on the back from the respectable. Every year or so in that decade, I self-published a book. Most were children's books to go with my school visits where I often did a book-signing after school and so had a ready market.

There were though big changes in the book trade afoot, especially helpful to self-published authors. There was print-on-demand; no longer would my bulging loft have to put up with thousands of copies, but just a few could be ordered when I needed them. About the same time came the ebook, which I thought would be ephemeral, but the Kindle's emergence in 2007 ensured its permanence.

From 2010

In this decade, my school visits began to tail off due to government cuts in education funding. Setbacks can be an opportunity. I turned to crime and began my *Jack of All*

Trades series. The first three were published in 2015. As I write this in 2019, there are now nine in the series, set where I live, with murders galore. They are in ebook and paperback editions. All the books are entitled Jack something or other. It's my marketing device. They are:

- *Jack of All Trades*
- *Jack of Spades*
- *Jack o'Lantern*
- *Jack By The Hedge*
- *Jack In The Box*
- *Jack On The Tower*
- *Jack Recalled*
- *Jack At Death's Door*
- *Jack At The Gate*

Jack is a builder who solves crimes. Wherever he works someone gets murdered. It is a wonder anyone employs him.

Teaching Experience

I taught Writing for Children for eighteen years, beginning at City University, then at the Mary Ward Centre in Holborn. I was co-ordinator of Newham Writers Workshop for twenty years, and have run poetry and general writing workshops in various places. In schools, from 1998 to 2016, I ran story-writing workshops in primary and secondary schools.

I am a member of the Society of Authors and the Crime Writers Association.

So that's me, warts and all, writing on, and about to share with you my experience of writing crime.

CHAPTER 2: What is a Crime Novel?

Here's my definition:

> A crime novel is a fictional story of 40 thousand or more words, intended to be read. One or more crimes, usually murder, are committed as the major element of the story.
>
> As well as a perpetrator, the story should have a detective, who may be professional or amateur, who will attempt to thwart the perpetrator's endeavours at evading punishment.

The play *Hamlet* has a murder (Hamlet's father) which is the major element of the story. It has a detective too (Hamlet). But it fails our definition as, although it is read, it is primarily intended for performance.

A Study in Scarlet, by Arthur Conan Doyle, is the first appearance of Sherlock Holmes. It is a novel of 40 thousand words. Some say that makes it a novella. As there is no precise boundary between novel and novella, I'm not going to make a fight of it. The book was published in 1887 and is still popular. If that doesn't help my case, it certainly doesn't harm it.

My crime novels are between 55 and 65 thousand words. On the short side perhaps, but what counts most of all is a good book. The crime must be a major element of the plot. In Charles Dickens' *Bleak House* there is a murder, but no one would suggest that it is a murder novel, as the death is part of a subplot.

Whether the investigation is successful or not I leave open in this definition, as there are a variety of endings. The perpetrators sometimes get away with it. I've allowed them to do it in *Jack of Spades*. In this case, those killed are a lot nastier than the perpetrators. Cowboy justice if you like. One though has to be fair on readers, and they know who did it even if the police don't.

There are, in fact, quite a few crime novels where the killer gets away with it. I have considered giving some examples other than my own, but I am reluctant to give spoilers. Suffice it to say, it happens in fiction, as in real life.

It used to be said, rather proudly, that 'the Mounties always get their man.' That's the Royal Canadian Mounted Police. And grand they look in their red jackets on horseback, but I am sceptical of this claim. I have no doubt, like any other police force, they made quite a few wrongful arrests. I am sure, too, they have unsolved crimes on their books.

Justice is inevitably imperfect. Good for crime writers, not so good for the wrongly convicted.

Crime or Mystery?

When I was a child of eight or nine, my mother would send me to the local library. She'd say, 'Get me a murder book.' So off I'd go with this instruction. At the library, among the books, I could often tell by the title alone if the book fitted the category. If it had the words 'Death' or 'Killing' or 'Murder' in it, that would fit the bill. Or the cover had a picture of a woman lying, blood splattered, on a carpet. Some had a gun on the spine. I was no judge of quality; I never bothered looking inside.

'Murder book' was an apt label for the type of book my mother wanted, but publishers and authors, being well brought up, require an appellation less bloody.

In the US the term 'mystery' is used. It stems from the time when most crime novels were mysteries, or whodunits. Sherlock Holmes and Agatha Christie presented the reader with a puzzle which we, the readers, would try to work out, given the clues and suspects. Usually though, the killer remained a mystery until the last chapter when it was explained to us by the clever detective.

But many books shoehorned into the mystery category are not mysteries at all. Good examples are Patricia Highsmith's Ripley novels, the first called *The Talented Mr Ripley*. Ripley is a killer and the reader knows it. A serial killer, in fact. There is no mystery about that, but you can still find it in the mystery section.

Beyond its history, the term 'mystery' has stuck for all murder books in some quarters. My preferred clarifier is 'crime'. There is always a crime committed, whether it is a mystery or not.

In the case of my *Jack of All Trades* series, nine books so far, three of them are not mysteries. One, *Jack in the Box*, features an armed siege, where Jack is one of the hostages. We know the hostage takers, so it's no mystery. In *Jack o'Lantern*, we follow the murderers doing the deed. The reader knows more than Jack and the police who believe the death to be accidental. The other non-mystery of mine is *Jack of Spades*. In this tale, we know the killers, even sympathise with them and hope they get away with it.

'Mystery' will continue to be used in some circles, however much I quibble. I've had to tick the mystery box myself on Amazon and Bookbub, an online book publiciser. They won't change their minds for me.

The Thriller

The essence of a thriller (sometimes called suspense novel) is that someone is trying to kill the main character. So the main character has to get the baddy before the baddy gets them. Well known examples are the James Bond books and the Bourne movies.

I will from time to time use films and TV as examples, as they are well known, and assist me in making my point. Many crime films and TV series started life as books. The adaptor for screen was sometimes the writer, but more often specialised script writers.

A crime novel may be a thriller. But not all thrillers are crime novels. The international and inter-governmental aspects rule out James Bond and Bourne in most definitions of crime novel. The crime novel is more parochial, mostly set in one place. The rule though is not hard and fast, as many crime novels have thriller elements, especially near the end when the killer is being hunted down. Killing the detective, the murderer may see as the only way to evade capture.

A single book or a series?

In 2011, I attended a writing festival, invited there as a children's author. At a library, there were three authors, including me, talking about their work, one of them a crime writer who had been writing in the genre for more than twenty years. He told the audience that with his first book, he began by putting his main characters in an almost impossible situation, and, knowing no more than that, he continued writing.

When I got back from the festival, I took a few of his books out of the library. I read them, and thought, he's an established crime writer, but I can do better. This is not an uncommon reaction for a writer. We wouldn't write at all without a little arrogance. I thought I'd use his trick of putting the main character in an almost impossible situation and see if I could write my way out of it.

The situation I thought up was:

> A young man wakes up in a bed, in a strange room, next to a naked, dead woman.

My knowledge was limited to that sentence. I didn't know who he was, who she was or even where he was. It was quite a problem to sort out, and my imagination turned somersaults. I decided it was a set-up. The young man, I called Jim Price. He had come to the house for a job but had been drugged, and was now about to be blackmailed by the house owner. The police would be called unless Jim killed the man's wife.

I sent Jim Price off to do the killing. On the edge of belief you might say, but not infrequent in the genre. And I finished up with a 26 thousand word novella, entitled *Murder at Any Price*.

It is a one-off, as it has nowhere else to go once everything is sorted out. The story of the main characters is done with as far as I was concerned. It was though useful for me to write, as it gave me the confidence to go on and plan the *Jack of All Trades* series.

I am in no way belittling standalone novels and suggesting they are all apprentice works. That's nonsense. Paula Hawkins' *The Girl on the Train* did extremely well as a book and as a film, and certainly launched her career. Her follow up, *Into the Water*, is another one-off. It sold well but the critics in general feel it is not as good as her first, so her next is crucial. This applies to series too. You have to keep the standard up, as one weak link can put readers off the rest.

The choice is yours: one-off or series. Though a one-off can be the beginning of a series, but often it can't be as too many doors have been shut. Most series writers are planning a series before they begin writing the first book.

The essence of a series is a main character in a specific setting. For example, Peter James' series, featuring Chief Superintendent Roy Grace, are set in Brighton. When one book is written, the author still has his main character, his colleagues and the setting to help him plan the next. And sometimes an ongoing subplot. Peter James had one with C/Supt Roy Grace's ex wife who disappeared, but like a ghost haunts the first books of the series.

A series has marketing advantages too. For example, Ian Rankin has written over twenty Inspector Rebus books. As soon as a new one comes out, readers are eager for it. They want to keep up with the hard drinking Edinburgh cop. Amazon lists books in a series together, so the reader can see where they have got to. If you have a Kindle and finish one of a series, Amazon will suggest you try the next.

Then again, John Grisham has written lots of standalone crime books, mostly featuring lawyers. He hasn't needed a series to bump him into the bestsellers' league.

With *Jack of All Trades* I decided from the outset I was going to write a series. I hadn't a title yet, just the inclination to write a crime series. My thinking was I would, hopefully, hook readers with the first book, so they would then go on to read more. For that I needed the right character and place. And some good storytelling.

But I am moving ahead of myself. We'll come back to planning a series, but now we'll consider personal taste.

Hard Boiled or Cozy?

For most writers, this sorts itself out naturally, being dependent on the writer's sensibility. You might though be somewhere down the middle like me.

A hard boiled crime novel has graphic violence, swearing and sex. The cozy has none of these. Well, not quite none, as you can't have a murder novel without violence, but in a cozy the violence happens off-stage. In classic crime, such as Agatha Christie's, a body is discovered in the library in the morning. The victim has been hit on the head with a blunt instrument. You get no more detail than that. In hard boiled crime, the reader is not spared the blood and gore. There may be torture, there may be rape, and the writer does not hold back on swearing.

I'm a three minute egg. My *Jack of All Trades* books do not dwell on the violence. I don't go in for rape, and my sex scenes are short. I originally had a fair bit of swearing in the first three books, as I am not averse to it. People swear in real life, I do a bit myself, but know when not to. I am safe in polite company.

We cannot avoid unpleasant characters in crime novels. A character might be racist, homophobic or anti-trans. This doesn't make the book racist or anti LGBT+, but you might consider getting a first reader (known as a beta reader) from that group to check that you are not giving unintended insults.

My first novel in the series, the eponymously titled *Jack of All Trades*, received a poor review on Amazon because of swearing. Another 20 ticked 'like'. The reviewer said she would have given me five stars but because of the swearing she was giving me three. That made me reflect. Did I need it? I hadn't really considered this aspect. I was writing the sort of book I would want to read. But including swearing, I would inevitably lose readers. And get bad reviews.

Would my books be impaired if I took out the swear words? I decided they wouldn't be, and removed the offending words. I had to get creative, no bad thing for a writer, to find expressions for, say, the f-word. Since the first three novels, which are now clean, I've kept swearing out. No critic has yet said, I have given this novel three stars, but might have given it five if there had been good, honest, down to earth, Anglo-Saxon swearing!

Points to consider

- Are you going to write a standalone or a series?
- Will your book be cozy, in-between, or hard-boiled?

EXERCISE 1

I started my novel, *Murder at Any Price*, with Jim Price in a difficult situation, namely:

Waking up in a bed, in a strange room, next to a naked, dead woman.

Invent a difficult situation for your main character. Just a few sentences will do. Beginning with that situation, write the next 500 words.

CHAPTER 3: Types of Crime Novels

I f you are thinking of starting a new business, you do your market research. Well, our new business is the crime novel. So let's examine the type of crime novels that people are reading as it will assist you in deciding which you want to write. Like a detective, at this stage, reject nothing.

There are a variety of ways of classifying crime novels, some more useful than others. You could for instance decide to do it by the crime. But very quickly you would find that 95% of those crimes are murders, with just 5% left over for robbery, kidnapping and other crimes. You would then have to think about sub-categories for murder, such as family murder, murder by strangers, serial killings. Family murder, being common, you would need to subdivide further into such sectors as murder of the wife by the husband, murder of the husband by the wife, murder of a parent, of a step parent, of a stepchild and so forth.

I have not used this scheme, as I didn't feel it would be that useful to a writer. The classification I offer is via the role of the main character. Without a good main character, any novel will be lifeless. They are the heart and soul of the book, more so in a series, captured in such phrases as 'the latest Inspector Rebus', 'a Wexford case', 'an Inspector Montalbano mystery'.

A word of caution. It is only a scheme, not the last word like the Periodic Table. Not every book will fit that well.

Some might fit two sectors, and if I settle on one, you may not agree. Fine, feel free to move it.

Enough provisos. Let's look at it.

Categories of Crime Fiction

- Police Procedurals: 70%
- Police Associates: 15%
- Private Eyes: 10%
- Workers: few %
- Accidental detective: few %
- Historical: few %
- Killers: few %

This list does not include true crime. Our brief is fiction. The sectors are based on the main character's role in the novel. There's one exception, Historical. Each of the above categories could have a sub-class called historical, when the author chose to set the novel(s) in the past. But a Tudor or medieval investigator has distinct differences from a modern one, so I have decided to have Historical as a category by itself.

The percentages are back of the envelope estimates, made up from my reading and perusing the local library shelves. There's scope here for a PhD thesis, but not for me. I don't need to be that accurate and I doubt you do. Unless you want to sign up for the PhD, if so, I'd be grateful for your stats.

Police Procedural

This is the biggest sector by far. A cop is the main character, nearly always a senior cop. We follow the police investigation of the crime through their eyes, with station politics very important. The cops often lead teams though they may be a maverick, like Rebus or Morse, both of whom hang onto their jobs because they catch criminals, not through their interpersonal skills.

70% for Police Procedurals is a big chunk of 100%. Rather too big. We can break it down by country. Being British, I'd sub-divide the sector into: British, US, European, and International Police Procedurals. You might say extracting British from European is somewhat parochial. Perhaps, but languages are barriers. I read in English, and that means I read British writers, US, and others who write in English. Non-English language novels, I can read only in translation.

Some British fictional cops are:

- Detective Inspector Rebus, Edinburgh, by Ian Rankin
- Detective Inspector Endeavour Morse, Oxford, by Colin Dexter
- Detective Chief Inspector Roy Grace, Brighton, by Peter James
- Chief Inspector Wexford, Kingsmarkham, Sussex, by Ruth Rendell
- Chief Inspector Adam Dalgliesh, London, by PD James
- Detective Chief Inspector Jane Tennison, London, by Lynda La Plante

The one exception I know of a cop in British crime fiction outside the higher ranks is Sophie Hannah's Detective Constable Simon Waterhouse. He is part of the Culver

Valley police force. Sophie Hannah says she invented this county because of the British obsession with class. She could do things there without someone writing to tell her that would never happen in Hampstead, Brighton, Edinburgh etc, as Culver Valley is fictitious.

One of the earliest cops in fiction is Inspector Bucket in Charles Dickens' *Bleak House*, published in episodes, in 1852 and 53. It is a meandering novel, featuring wills and their ensuing court cases that go on forever. And where there's a will, there's a murder, in fiction at least. A BBC series, Dickensian, running in 2016 resurrected Inspector Bucket.

US Police Procedurals

There are a host of these. I have made an idiosyncratic selection.

Ed McBain wrote the 87th Precinct series, set in New York, focusing on Detective Steve Carella. McBain was very prolific, writing for nearly 50 years up to his death in 2005.

Michael Connelly's detective is the fancily-named Hieronymus Bosch, known more familiarly as Harry, an LAPD detective. These novels are not cozy. Well, you couldn't be on the mean streets of Los Angeles.

James Patterson is a bestselling author whose sleuth is Alex Cross, a psychologist who became disillusioned with the 'science' and its expense for people who need its expertise. So he became a cop in Washington DC, shooting and analysing. Mostly in the right order.

Karin Slaughter has agent Will Trent as her cop in the Georgia Bureau of Investigation, Atlanta. Trent was brought up in an orphanage, so he had lots to overcome in growing up. He's dyslexic too, and goes to great lengths to disguise his trouble with reading. Will solves crimes but doesn't get on with the team. My kind of cop, I prefer them with problems.

James Lee Burke goes down south with Dave Robicheaux as deputy sheriff in Iberia, Louisiana. Robicheaux rarely plays by the book, a somewhat wild law enforcer. He is a recovering alcoholic who suffers bouts of depression brought on by his military experience and troubled upbringing in rural Louisiana. You get the pattern. Troubled cops are more interesting for authors and readers.

Jeffrey Deaver has Lincoln Rhyme as his detective. He is ex-NYPD but was invalided out. Every so often he is called in to assist his former colleagues.

Julie Smith has New Orleans as her setting with her detective, Skip Langdon. Skip is somewhat upper crust, her family knowing all the right people. Skip though has an enemy, a nasty preacher Jacomine, out to get her if she can't get him first.

I could go on, as this is the tiniest of fractions of US police procedurals, but my intention is just to give the flavour and pass on the message: make your cop interesting.

International Cops

Maj Sjöwall and Per Wahlöö, a married couple, wrote the Martin Beck series between the 1960s and 1970s. Beck is a cop in the National Homicide Department of Stockholm. I have enjoyed these recently on TV. They planned the books together and then wrote alternate chapters. Afterwards, they'd swap chapters for editing. Ten books had been written when Per died in 1975.

George Simenon, a Belgian, wrote the Inspector Maigret novels. Maigret is a Paris cop, each novel written in less than ten days. Simenon wrote close to 200 novels, 150 novellas and countless articles. How he had time for his claimed 10,000 women, I can't say.

Jo Nesbo is a Norwegian writer. His cop, Harry Hole, is a member of the Oslo police department. He battles with alcoholism and depression. Nesbo has his way out: he is the main vocalist and songwriter for the Norwegian rock band Di Derre.

Inspector Kurt Wallander, another Scandi-noir creation, is the brainchild of Swedish writer Henning Mankell. The tales are set around the town of Ystad, south-east of Malmö. Wallander reminds me of Morse, both characters love opera and are somewhat friendless.

Inspector Montalbano is Andrea Camilleri's Sicilian cop in the imaginary town of Vigàta. He hates having his meal interrupted, even for a murder. A keen swimmer from his beachside house, but not straight after lunch. Food is to be enjoyed. A welcome antidote to our fast food nation. I have enjoyed the TV series based on the novels.

A favourite author of mine is Louise Penny, a Canadian writer. Her detective is Chief Inspector Armand Gamache of the Sûreté du Québec. He lives in the village of Three Pines which is surprisingly lively for a village not even on the map, with a bistro, a bed and breakfast and a bookshop. Gamache is regularly off to Montreal to sort out crime and corrupt cops.

Another favourite is Tana French with her Dublin Murder Squad. One of whom is Detective Antoinette Conway. She swears to shock a trooper, she's more than difficult, and only her sidekick puts up with her, but she solves crimes. An outsider makes a good main character. The happily married and untroubled are somewhat bland and indistinguishable.

A TV series to be included here is CSI, a popular TV series, easy to catch up on as its repeats are myriad among the host of channels. Crime scene investigators are cops usually, who are to be seen on hands and knees going studiously over the area where someone has been found dead. They are togged in paper or plastic suits, with hoods, masks and plastic gloves. The purpose of the gear is to avoid contaminating the scene with their own DNA, fingerprints, clothing fibres etc.

In real life crime, OJ Simpson was charged with murdering his wife Nicole and her friend Ron Goldman in 1994. Much criticism has been made of how contaminated the crime scene was by multiple coming and goings by the police. OJ was acquitted, and the contaminated scene was a factor, though just as much was the racism of the LA police force.

Police Procedurals are popular, and so the sector is a fertile ground for you. But it is not the only ground.

Police Associates

My estimate is that fifteen per cent of crime novels have main characters who are involved with crime because of their work with the law. They may be lawyers, coroners, pathologists etc.

John Grisham often has a lawyer as the lead character in his novels. Though, quite often, they are at loggerheads with the cops. That's lawyers for you. He has done very well as a best selling author for many years without having a series.

Patricia Cornwell has her medical examiner, Dr. Kay Scarpetta. Scarpetta was initially Chief Medical Examiner for Virginia before becoming a consultant medical examiner. There's lots of forensic examination of corpses, but Scarpetta spends much of her time outside the mortuary, more like a private eye, which is not true to life but readers don't complain, even if real medical examiners have their gripes.

In a similar vein, on TV, we have Silent Witness, a BBC crime drama focusing on the investigations of a team of forensic pathologists. They work closely with the police, but do a surprising amount of work outside the laboratory, investigating crimes which often gets them into dire straits.

Quite understandable, as a lab based series wouldn't last long.

Dr Ruth Galloway is a forensic archaeologist from the pen of Elly Griffiths. There's a stretch, you may well think, to archaeology. Galloway deals with cold cases, sometimes ultra cold. Galloway lives in a seaside cottage in Norfolk and teaches at the University of North Norfolk. She has a complicated relation with DCI Nelson with whom she had a child. He is her ear to the police investigation, though often uncomfortably.

Kathy Reichs is a renaissance woman. She is a novelist, a forensic anthropologist and academic, and also has three children. Quite how she holds it all together, I wonder, though they do say if you want something done – give it to a busy woman. Her fictional anthropologist is Temperance Brennan. There is some irony in that first name, as Brennan has an alcohol problem. The science is dead right, but as is common with such novels, Tempe spends a lot of time outside the lab investigating.

Frieda Klein is the creation of the husband-and-wife couple making up Nicci French (Sean French and Nicci Gerrard). I am in awe as to how they do it, as the writing is of high quality and seamless. Klein is a psychotherapist (what else with a name like that?) who lives in London. She is fascinated by London's underground rivers and takes long walks in the early hours. Through the series she gets involved with a number of investigations involving murders and kidnapping. The police use her skills, but then wish they hadn't. A highly recommended series.

So far, Police Procedurals and Police Associates cover 85% of crime novels. That leaves us with 15%.

Keep up.

Private Eyes

The next ten per cent are private investigators. There are amateurs and there are professionals. Amateurs are less common these days as you need a private income. The first amateur, in fact the first detective in fiction, is Chevalier Auguste Dupin in Edgar Allan Poe's 1841 short story *Murders in the Rue Morgue*. Dupin uses the analytical method we are familiar with from Sherlock Holmes and Hercule Poirot. Poe's story is told by an unnamed narrator, a friend of Dupin's, reminiscent of Watson, the narrator of the Sherlock Holmes tales. Dupin solves the case for his own amusement. Very amateur, and with blundering police too.

Agatha Christie's Poirot, a Belgian, has no money problems, and is in and out of large English country houses. Miss Marple, by the same author, lives in the village of St. Mary Mead and is happy to be called in to solve a murder or two, often for a friend or a friend of a friend. And of course to put the police right. Money is never mentioned by either, nor by Lord Peter Wimsey, Dorothy L Sayers' sleuth. He is filthy rich and wouldn't dream of asking for cash.

That's a brief look at the amateurs. Let's look at those investigators who have to make money to live.

Sherlock Holmes refers to himself as a consulting detective. He takes a fee from his clients, though he'll work for expenses if he likes the case. When working for royalty or the government, he's amply rewarded to compensate for his discounted cases. Watson and Holmes came together because Holmes could not afford the Baker Street rooms on his own in his early days as a consulting detective.

Philip Marlowe is Raymond Chandler's investigator for hire. His manor is Los Angeles, where he has a dusty office. He drinks whisky and brandy, smokes Camels but also plays chess and went to college for a few years. Streetwise but not unlettered. My image of him comes via his portrayal by

Humphrey Bogart in such film noir classics as *The Big Sleep* with Lauren Bacall.

More recently, there's Cormoran Strike, cut from the same cloth, who is Robert Galbraith's detective. Galbraith is better known as JK Rowling, not short of money herself, but her PI has to sleep in the office. He lost half a leg in his military service in Afghanistan and there's too many stairs up to his office. His partner is Robin, whose husband is irritated by Strike and tells her continually she can make twice the money elsewhere. But she prefers the exciting life.

We have the No 1 Ladies' Detective Agency by Alexander McCall Smith. McCall Smith's private eye is the astute Mma Precious Ramotswe, the first female private eye in Botswana. She has a living to make but also must battle with men who think this is not suitable work for a woman.

Vaseem Khan has ex-Inspector Chopra, formerly of the Mumbai Police, as his main character. On retirement Chopra sets up his own agency, the Baby Ganesha Agency. His sidekick is a baby elephant, a remarkably astute animal, working with Chopra in various cases amidst the corruption and inequalities of Mumbai.

Sara Paretsky's sleuth is V. I. Warshawski. Her patch is Chicago. She's educated, sporty, and stylish. She deals mostly with white collar crime, often with the powerful, and may come up with half a result. That's private eyes for you; there's only so much they can do.

Workers

We're down to the last 5% of crime novels. We've eliminated cops, police associates (legals, medicals etc) and private eye main characters. Now we have the workers; those who through their job come across murders.

There's Lily Bard, Charlaine Harris's sleuth, who works in Shakespeare in Arkansas. Lily is a cleaner, lying low in

Shakespeare to get away from a much publicised rape she suffered in Memphis. She's an ace at martial arts and needs to be, considering some of the lowlifes she has to deal with.

An earlier series by the same author has as its heroine Aurora Teagarden. She is a librarian to begin with, but ventures into real estate. She belongs to the Real Murders Club which investigates unsolved cases in Lawrenceton, Georgia. A number of US writers have used realtors as their protagonists. There are lots of possibilities with the various properties on the market. It's almost a subgenre in itself. Aurora Teagarden crosses my categories. When she finds a body in her realtor work, she's a Worker. But with the Real Murders Club, you might list her as an amateur private eye.

Rebecca Tope, a British writer, has as her main character a florist, Persimmon Brown who owns a shop in Ambleside in the Lake District. She does floral displays in churches for christening, halls for weddings, and cemeteries for funerals. All significant events in our lives, and ripe settings for murder.

Lawrence Block has a fascinating character in Bernie Rhodenbarr. Bernie owns a bookshop, fine so far, but he is also a burglar by night. Sometimes, though, he climbs through the wrong window and becomes prime suspect for murder. And has to be the detective to get himself off the hook.

Elly Griffiths deserves another outing for her fine period series set in Brighton of the early 1950s. Her detective is the Great Mephisto, a stage magician, who works closely with his cop friend, Detective Inspector Edgar Stephens. I like the feel of the period and of variety theatre which is already feeling the pinch of television.

The Accidental Detective

This is the tale of someone who through bad luck becomes a detective. Their spouse might be murdered or kidnapped, or a son or daughter, a brother or sister. And they seek the killer. They will follow various clues and get closer and closer. Of course, as they close in on the killer, their own life becomes endangered. It is the old cowboy plot, except in that scenario the cowboy will be out to shoot the murderer. In the crime novel, the police will get involved at some point. It is likely to be a one-off as once the killer is arrested (or killed) the main character's motivation is assuaged.

Maddy Webb, in Jonathan Freedland's *The 3rd Woman*, is a journalist, and insomniac, whose sister is murdered. As the police are bungling the investigation, she is determined to find the killer. The setting is a strange one: an alternative-history USA so much in debt to the Chinese that there is a large Chinese garrison in LA where the novel is set.

In John Hart's *The Last Child*, set in North Carolina, thirteen-year-old Johnny Merrimon is hunting for his twin sister, Alyssa, who disappeared over a year ago. Everyone but him thinks she's dead. Alone and miserable, he sets out to find her.

In *The Analyst* by John Katzenbach, Dr. Frederick Starks, a New York psychoanalyst, gets a threatening letter from someone styling himself Rumplestiltskin. He will kill Starks' loved ones in two weeks unless Starks can guess who he is.

Killers

These are crime novels where the main character is the killer, and this is not hidden from the reader. A problem for the writer is that the main character needs to be someone likeable. If we think the killer is nothing but a hideous psychopath, we may well stop reading.

Patricia Highsmith's Ripley series *(The Talented Mr. Ripley, Ripley Under Ground, Ripley's Game, The Boy Who Followed Ripley, and Ripley Under Water)* have Tom Ripley as the killer conman. Will he get away with it? is the question we ask in each of the novels. *Strangers on a Train* is another of Highsmith's, when two strangers meet on a train and conspire to kill each other's wife.

Crime and Punishment, Dostoyevsky's classic novel, fits the bill. Raskolnikov is the killer of a mean money lender. He kills her half sister too as she caught him with the axe. We follow him all the way, from St Petersburg to Siberia in this tale of evil and redemption.

Historical

By historical, I don't mean characters like Sherlock Holmes, whose tales, first written in the late 1880s by Arthur Conan Doyle, are now period pieces. Or Lord Peter Wimsey, Dorothy L Sayers' sleuth, much of which was written in the 1920s. They weren't historical at the time of writing. I am referring to recent crime books set in the past.

A good example is Lindsey Davis' ancient Rome series. Marcus Didius Falco is her sleuth, a spy, with domestic problems as well as having mysteries to solve. The stories are earthy, and surprisingly hard boiled, and cover much of the Roman Empire, from Greece to Britannia. Davis has another series featuring Falco's daughter, Flavia Albia, who like her father, takes on cases no one else will touch.

Brother Cadfael is the sleuth in a series of novels by Ellis Peters. Cadfael is a 12th century Benedictine monk in Shrewsbury. Before becoming a monk in his 40s, he had a wild life as a sailor and soldier. He is a herbalist and keen observer of human nature, base and otherwise, who is called upon by his Abbot to find the truth in various cases.

Andrew Martin's railway detective, Jim Stringer, is a member of the North Eastern Railway Police. The series is set in the first decades of the 20th century. In one book, Stringer goes to the Somme in WWI to investigate a case, a single death amongst so many.

To Conclude

I have taken you on a journey through crime fiction, as a new writer needs to know what's out there. We learn from others and go on from where others have left off. You may want to do a police procedural. There's room, but lots of competition too. How will you make your police detective stand out from the crowd?

You may have specialist knowledge, say in the law, medicine, or maybe in an area not usually associated with crime. There is still virgin territory for sleuths. A farmer perhaps in a rural community. Priests have been done; we have Cadfael and GK Chesterton's Father Brown stories, but how about a Rabbi or an Imam? Or a teacher in a large secondary school. There would be other teachers to call on for their expertise, and school labs too. Kids could help out in internet searches, and following suspects. I am talking myself into it.

Above all, while you are on the lookout, read crime fiction, lots of it. Consider it your market research, as you home in on your patch.

EXERCISE 2

List 5 crime novels you have read. Say whether they are cozy, hard boiled or in-between. Which of the categories below best fits each one?

- Police Procedural
- Police Associates
- Private Eyes (amateur or profes-sional?)
- Workers
- Accidental detective
- Historical
- Killers

CHAPTER 4: Turning to Crime

S o there you are, all at sea, with all these possibilities for a crime novel. All those writers already doing it. What area shall you go for? A one-off or a series? A police procedural, a private eye, historical? Take it a step at a time.

This is what I did.

Why crime?

In 2013, I decided to write a series. When it comes to a series, the possible genres are: crime, romance, fantasy and science fiction. So theoretically, there were four major areas open to me. But you shouldn't write what you don't read. And I don't read much romance, fantasy or science fiction. I do read crime and have done since I was a teenager. I read my mother's Agatha Christie novels, and lapped up Sherlock Holmes. In later years, Nicci French and Louise Penny topped my list before I really got down to reading crime in order to write it.

I've watched a lot of TV crime. It's somewhat overdone on the box, there's good and bad. I have seen many crime movies. So a crime book wasn't a hard choice. Or even a choice at all.

Why a Series?

I figured if I was going to get a reputation as a crime writer, and make any money from it, a series would be more effective than one-offs. You may regard that as somewhat mercenary. It is. Samuel Johnson wrote, 'No man but a blockhead ever wrote except for money.' Well, I have certainly been a blockhead in my time and written quite a bit for not very much. This time, I was going to take the gold rush trail.

A series also gives you somewhere to go after the first book. You have a main character and those around them, you have a setting. So the second book isn't a blank page.

Why not a police procedural?

This is the most popular avenue of crime fiction. But I am not all that comfortable with the police. They are a state army, and in certain countries have behaved abominably. According to Amnesty International, 141 countries in the world use torture as an instrument of justice. That's a high proportion of the 195 countries in the UN. Dictatorships have fearful police systems where, once arrested, you are tortured to confess. To be arrested is to be guilty.

In the year 2000, Illinois suspended the death penalty due to growing evidence from DNA tests that innocent people had been executed for murders they had not committed. The police were part of the justice system that executed the innocent. They collected the evidence and, it is suspected, fabricated some of it. In 2014 Illinois finally gave up the death penalty. We have no idea worldwide how many innocent people are executed on police evidence. Or how many innocent people are in jail for crimes they didn't commit.

In the UK in the 1990s, the Stephen Lawrence affair illustrated the extent of racism in the police. Lawrence was an 18-year-old black youngster who was murdered in South London in 1993 in a racist attack. The police response was bungled. A 1998 public inquiry, headed by Sir William Macpherson, examined the original investigation and concluded that the force was institutionally racist. Many people believe the police remain racist. In the US, we have Black Lives Matter, an ongoing protest against the large number of black people shot by the police.

The Netherlands' police force co-operated too eagerly with the Nazis during World War II. They were paid a bonus for each Jew they sent to the death camps. So they sent the largest proportion of Jews, of any Western European country, to their deaths. When police go wrong, they really go wrong.

There is the other side of the coin. A country without a police force is hell for ordinary people. It is a country run by gangs with guns, where life is short, with routine killings and rape. It follows that a civilized country must have a police force, albeit under democratic control.

In the UK, PACE, the Police and Criminal Evidence Act of 1984 and updated since, was brought in to regulate police activity. It brought in such reforms as recording interviews and other measures to prevent the police doctoring their notebooks, individually or collectively.

Nevertheless, a nightmare of mine is to be arrested by the police, and to be wrongly accused of murder. My defence would depend on how much money I had to pay for a lawyer to fight my case. With no money, I'd get a lawyer of sorts, not that qualified, not that good. If I were rich (I am not), I could get a top lawyer. In the meantime, I'd be banged up, hoping the police would check out my alibi and follow up other suspects.

There's a tale I could write. But it wouldn't be a police procedural.

There is a footnote to my rejection of the police procedural. Writing my *Jack of All Trades* series, I have included a number of police characters. And one of them, Detective Sergeant Fayyad Kamani, I am mulling over whether to make him the lead in a novel.

Nothing is forever.

Why not a private eye?

I find this harder to answer. I have nothing against private eyes, but they just didn't energise me. I couldn't get excited at the prospect. Maybe I could force it? But that's not a good idea. With writing you have to feel some fervour, especially if the endeavour is going to last several years (six so far). Yes, you can push yourself and write pulp, but that wasn't my aim.

Writing shouldn't be drudgery. If it is, then the writing is not likely to be much good. A proviso here, some writers have done it when money was the factor. Arthur Conan Doyle killed off Sherlock Holmes as he was finding writing the stories a chore. They were overshadowing everything else he wrote. Four years later, he brought him back; money and acclaim I suspect were his motives.

Over the years, I have become more adept at knowing whether a novel is working. The most important feeling is the excitement to get on with it. When I feel the characters in the story. And I just couldn't see me doing that with a private eye.

I won't rule out this option. I might go there one day. Since I made the initial decision in 2013, I've read a lot more crime fiction. Barbara Nadel has her private eye partnership of Lee and Mumtaz, who have an office, a fictional one, about a mile from where I live. And I've liked what she's done. I enjoy the series by Robert Galbraith (JK Rowling) featuring Cormoran Strike. My favourite though is Jackson

Brodie, Kate Atkinson's Edinburgh private eye, but she seems to have left him behind. A pity for me, maybe not for her.

A private eye may come. Am I talking myself into it? I have no political objections. So maybe, maybe. But it had no heat at all in 2013.

So why Jack?

I did not dwell for a moment on lawyers or pathologists. My experience of these professionals was limited to TV and reading. Not that this needed to have stopped me, but I had no impetus to send me down that track.

I could see the attraction of historic crime, but boy, what a lot of research you need to do to convince the reader they are in the 16th century. All that before you've written a word of story. Often, the writers know the period well, before they start writing crime.

Not for me.

So rejecting again, I was down to workers. What job might my main character do that would take him to various settings where a murder might take place? You may note, I'd already decided on a male protagonist.

I didn't at any time consider a female main character. It simply did not cross my mind. I instinctively pressed the male button. In retrospect, this is somewhat worrying. I am less rational than I like to think I am.

The reason why I chose a man, instinctive or not, is clear enough. It was identification. Someone whose shoes I could comfortably fit in. And a male main character did that for me.

A male worker then. But what work?

I did my research in the local library. What other writers have had workers as their main character? I didn't find many. There was Bernie, the New York burglar, when he wasn't running a bookshop, Lily the cleaner in Shakespeare, Arkansas, Persimmon in her Lake District flower shop, and Aurora the librarian with her Real Murders club. Not many at all, but enough to tell me, it was a runner.

I came up with a builder. How did I? A number of factors came together. I don't know lawyers and pathologists but my father was a carpenter, working in the building trade for a time. I have known various builders. Maybe all the building work on my street, all the guys up on the scaffolding, on rooftops, drilling and hammering, were making their play in my head.

I did feel a certainty once I had homed in on a builder.

Jack Bell is his name. I have accompanied him to various settings as he travels about getting work. I have been with him on a variety of jobs: in houses, in a school, a park, and a cemetery. I had to do more research than I'd initially envisaged, as he must come across as a believable builder. And I am not a builder or even a DIY enthusiast. I will reluctantly get out a drill when a shelf is falling off the wall, but not before.

Jack is not well educated. He couldn't wait to leave school, but he is far from stupid. In his work, he has to assess a job, price it, buy materials, deal with any problems that come up, and of course have the various skills needed in his building work. It seems unfair to lumber him with murder investigations on top of all this, but that's my job.

I noted in my research that there is a dearth of working class sleuths. It was never my mission to put that right. I just got there somehow. But it is interesting to consider the reason for their paucity. Most writers are middle class, and writers tend to choose main characters they identify with. But the baddies and lowlifes – well, they can be working class, or would be working if they weren't scrounging. So we get a snobbish aversion to having them as detectives.

Consider challenging yourself. As maybe I should have done with the male/female decision. But in the end, you are the writer and you want a main character that you are happy with. Male, female, black, white, gay, straight, able bodied, disabled, and a host of nationalities. So many choices. And some of them, most of us make too instinctively.

And so

Your main character is paramount. Do have a good think. It doesn't pay to skimp on research. You may be living with him or her for quite a few years. Six years so far for me, and I haven't finished yet.

It's no less difficult for a one-off. The novel is going to take up a large chunk of your life. There will be lots of other things you can't do because you have to write. Homing in on your protagonist is imperative if your book is going to be any good.

It's character and story that grip the reader.

CHAPTER 5: Telling a Story

So down to basics. You are going to write a crime novel. You have sorted out your category. So you need a story. But hang about. What *is* a story?

A Story?

In 1998 I began visiting schools as a children's writer. At the time, I had only four children's books published and thought, I can't talk about them all day. So I had a think, and decided I would offer story-writing workshops.

I began planning these workshops. The question I immediately came up with was: what's a story? And found such an obvious question less than obvious. We all recognise a story. We tell them to each other, read them in books and newspapers, online, see them on TV and in the cinema, but it is not readily apparent what one actually is.

That struck me as important. There was a conundrum here which I needed to understand, apart from the fact that a child was bound to ask me, and I had to have the answer off pat. Before you read my definition, you may like to put this book down and have a go yourself.

EXERCISE 3

The surprising thing was that by 1998 I had been writing for thirty years, plays, short stories and novels, and had not once posed the question to myself. It was too obvious. Everyone knows what a story is.

No, they don't. Since '98 I have posed the question many times, to adults as well as children, and few of them give me the right answer. I get answers like: *it has a beginning, middle and end.* To which I reply: so does a length of string. Or – *it's a plot.* To which I say, that is another way of saying a story is a story. Or even, *it's a piece of writing.* Well, so is a car manual.

You may have the definition by now. Here's mine:

A story is about a character with a problem that is in some way resolved.

At which point, you slap yourself on the forehead and say, of course. Like I did. A character of course must be present. You can't possibly have a story without a character. It doesn't have to be human, or even an animal, it could be a leaf, a raindrop, but if you go for the non-living you will anthropomorphise them, that is give them human characteristics. Like Old Man River or Mother Nature.

40

A character alone won't do. They could be walking down the street. That's not a story, until a bike comes off the road and hits them. There has to be a problem. It is surprising how many supposed stories haven't got a problem. They meander all over the place, not knowing where they are going. There are so-called plotless novels, like James Joyce's *Ulysses*, but these actually break up into a number of stories.

Let's consider the resolution of the story. There has to be some sort of ending. Or it's half a story. The ending could be happy, unhappy, or even death, but some sort of ending is needed to complete the story.

One of the most popular genres is the romance. The problem is clear, the lovers want to get together but something is stopping them. Could be a parent, class, race or a religious barrier. They will get together in the end in a typical romance, as opposed to a Romeo and Juliet type. The reader wants a happy ending, and will complain if this is not realised.

In our genre, crime, the problem leaps out. It is of course the crime itself, usually a murder. There may be subplots which lead up to it, say romance or a difficulty with the detective's home life, but the major problem for the main character is the murder. They might be the cop investigating it, or a suspect, or wrongly-accused, or a private eye called in, a one-time-only detective and so forth. In one way or another the murder is their problem. Whether as a job, as a suspect, or reluctant detective, the murder forces them onwards.

So we have a character with a problem. Keep that in mind. But if the story is any good, the problem must be hard to solve. If it is easy to solve then it's a poor story. Like the love story, there must be obstacles in the way that the detective has to surmount.

Let's look at fairy tales, a detour on our story odyssey. Or is it? Most fairy stories are crime stories, with a baddy, often a serial killer, who has to be overcome by the goody.

That's the basic plot of many a crime story too. A little skimpy perhaps, but let's see how we can give it more structure by a critical analysis of *Little Red Riding Hood*.

The Big Bad Wolf, the baddy of the tale, meets Little Red Riding Hood in the forest on her way to Grandma's cottage. He stops her for a chat, as one would. If he had eaten her then and there, with the main character dead, the story is over and done with. It is a lousy tale. It has no middle, just a beginning and a rushed end.

Though, we could make a decent story of it if we make the wolf the main character. Then, Ripley-style, this could be the first of the wolf's many killings. And on goes the tale. Depending how you do it, it could be popular with children, especially if most of the victims are grown ups. If he chases LRRH off for instance, and just eats adults. Say teachers and cops. I am thinking of Roald Dahl and some of his less approved of main characters.

Or consider *Punch & Judy*, a popular puppet show in the UK, most often seen at the seaside. Punch is a serial killer, killing the baby, his wife and the cop who comes to get him. I recall when I was a kid, when we still had the death penalty in the UK, Punch even got the hangman to demonstrate how he should put his head in the noose. Goodbye, hangman. All this, so forbidden. I loved it!

As I haven't seen a Punch & Judy show for many years, I looked it up while writing this book. It's still going strong, though schools have banned it. Current shows have been cleaned up, but I found this quote:

The story of Mr Punch is that he kills his baby, then his wife Judy and the police officer who comes to arrest him. He outwits a ghost, a crocodile and a doctor, convinces the hangman to be hanged in his place and, at the play's end, even defeats the devil himself.

Tom Ripley, you are a wimp compared to Mr Punch.

Making the Problem Hard to Solve

Back to *Little Red Riding Hood*. The story so far: LRRH is on her way to Grandma's with a basket of goodies. She has been warned not to speak to anyone on her way through the forest. Now read on.

But the Big Bad Wolf intercepts her, and she inadvertently tells the wolf she is going to Grandma's. The wolf sprints ahead. His aim is to eat them both at his leisure in Grandma's cottage. With these traditional additions, the story now has a beginning, middle and end.

Note, it was necessary to keep LRRH alive. Killing off your main character is bad practice.

Three Goes

The baddy in a fairy tale has to be beaten, but not too easily. One popular way of making it less than easy is what I call 'three goes'.

In the *Three Little Pigs,* the wolf has *three* goes at the pigs in their houses. In one popular telling, the pigs in the first two houses run to the third house, the one of bricks, where we have the showdown. That's how the problem is made hard to solve. Straw, sticks, bricks. (Say that quickly with a cracker in your mouth.)

Jack goes up the beanstalk three times, coming back down, consecutively, with the hen, the harp and the gold coins, before the giant spots him. Ali Baba has three wishes, Hansel and Gretel go three times into the woods before getting lost. The Three Billy Goats Gruff each have to cross the Troll's bridge, one at a time. Three times is awfully common in fairy tales.

We could steal that mode for our crime novel.

How it might go

Within your novel, there will be a murder and all sorts of obstacles before the murderer is caught. There could be three suspects, each one in turn is most certainly the killer. Until the first is murdered (Agatha Christie style), the second is now prime suspect, until she is bumped off in turn. And we are left with the real villain, who will try to kill the detective. I doubt they'll succeed. Most likely, after some cliff hanging dramatics, they'll be arrested. Alternatively, they could escape and appear, perhaps under another guise, in the second novel of your series.

EXERCISE 4

Your character is a killer. He has three people to kill. Come up with a reason why.

He sets off to kill the first one. Write 500 words from your killer's viewpoint.

CHAPTER 6: Place

Many crime novels are set in a real place. Inspector Rebus is an Edinburgh cop, Morse is in Oxford, Bernie the bookseller/burglar is in New York City, V I Warshawski is in Chicago, ex-Inspector Chopra has Mumbai. All distinctive cities.

With the *Jack of All Trades* series, I had written the first three books but had no specific setting. They were probably in London, but I didn't actually say so. None had been published at that time, as I was working with an agent to get them traditionally published. But I got impatient as I read more about the opportunities for self-publishing in the digital age, and took them back.

Between writing each of the three books, I set aside time for reading. Mostly crime. And I became more aware of place. Not surprisingly, I was in the right frame of mind to note what other crime writers were doing.

I hadn't fixed a place for the series. But it wasn't too late, as none had been published. I considered where the setting might be. And thought, why not round here? Forest Gate, where I have lived for over thirty years. It is a multi-ethnic area of East London, with about forty thousand people.

I went through each of the books and did the appropriate rewriting to set them around here. Jack Bell, my main character, lives on Earlham Grove in Forest Gate. I too live on that road. How convenient, you might say. He lives about fifty yards away. His address is:

Jack Bell
76b Earlham Grove
Forest Gate
London E7

I could give you the full postcode, but there isn't much point, as 76b Earlham Grove doesn't exist. For some reason, the numbers on Earlham Grove jump from 72 to 78. In between are a shed and a long garden wall. Should you attempt to post him a letter, for some work perhaps, you will befuddle the postie. Though I would appeal to you, please don't employ Jack. You might think this strange, that I should be so unhelpful but I am only thinking of your health. Be warned. People get murdered where he works.

That is an absurdity of course. Why would anyone employ a builder when people are regularly getting bumped off on his jobs? In short, they wouldn't. So I have instituted a sort of amnesia from book to book. Neither Jack, the police nor anyone else in the books recalls that there were murders where Jack last worked. Not that Jack killed them, I hasten to add, but he does seem to attract the wrong sort.

The advantages of a specific place

I have had several launches of the books in Forest Gate library. They cost me nothing and I sell signed copies of the paperbacks. I am a local author so the library might have allowed me a launch anyway, but as the books are set in Forest Gate they were obliged to, more or less.

I have built up a local fan base which is useful for future launches and other events. I have a bookstall at Forest Gate Festival, which is in July each year, where I have all my Jacks and my children's books for sale. They are the only books on the stall.

Local readers like it when streets they know, the shops, coffee bars, the library etc are in the story. And they will seek out the next book when it is published. I have also had correspondence from people who used to live in Forest Gate and moved away, and are pleased that the places they remember come up in my fiction.

I use actual places in the stories, sometimes as a main setting. In a house on nearby Claremont Road I arranged an armed siege (*Jack in the Box*) with Jack as one of the hostages. The cemetery, for example, where Jack is employed to build a memorial bower (*Jack at Death's Door*) is based on the local one. Several times, I went to visit it which helped with the writing, another advantage of using places you know.

The shops, streets, parks etc are familiar to you, and you can imagine your characters in that setting. Go visit them, take your note book, see who else is there. What's the weather like?

There are recurring places. The Forest Cafe, a greasy spoon, where Jack sometimes has lunch. Not far off is Wanstead Flats which is an area with football pitches and scrubland. Jack has a telescope and goes there on clear evenings, sometimes with his daughter, Mia.

In the first couple of books, I took him out to a hill by Epping Forest with his telescope. It's ten miles away. I decided there was no need to go that far. Keep it local.

Jack living in my area helps with ideas. I went to visit a woman about a year ago, who runs a guest house on Earlham Grove, where we both live. And I thought, yes, a guest house! I'll use that. I've peopled it with guests and a landlady. One to be murdered, the rest to be the suspects. Jack is there to make a concrete base for a shed and to assemble it. And to solve the crime when it occurs.

Not all crime writers use real places. As I have noted elsewhere, Sophie Hannah decided against a specific place, as she didn't want any arguments as to the class of the area. With a fictional place, like her Culver Valley, only the author has the answers. Charlaine Harris has Lily Bard living in Shakespeare, Arkansas. The US state is real enough, the town is not. Andrea Camilleri has Inspector Montalbano living in Sicily, in the fictitious seaside town of Vigàta.

Making up a town, you won't get accused of getting a place wrong. Not to start with, though you might contradict yourself once you get, say, to the seventh in the series. But to begin with you have virgin territory with buildings, politics and people.

Historical crime novels use places that were once real. Brother Cadfael lived in 12th century Shrewsbury. Ellis Peters, the author of the series, grew up nearby, but modern Shrewsbury bears little resemblance to its 12th century embodiment. She had to research the area through museums, books and ancient maps. She could, though, take liberties, with few to chastise her.

I stick to the present, and have found setting the series locally beneficial. It helps with marketing and settings for plots. There's only one disadvantage I can think of. The present changes and you may end up with some anachronisms. For example, Jack meets someone in CoffeE7. That cafe closed in 2017. In another book, Jack goes past the old West Ham football stadium in Upton Park and remarks on the building work there. I really should have anticipated that one, as the building work has morphed into apartment blocks.

I am not stuck with Forest Gate. If I want to take Jack out of the area, I can readily come up with a reason. He is, after all, a builder with a van. I need just give him some work in the other setting, get a group of people together, and kill someone.

Specific places are the default in crime series. Less so in one-offs, but Ruth Rendell in her one-offs often used London locations. In an interview, she said she would walk the streets to get to know the buildings and the people round about. Take her tip. If you are using a real place, go walk about, you'll see much more than out of a car window. You can sit on a wall and write your notes. Take your time.

My two young adult crime novels are also set in real locations. *Hard Cash*, I set in a block of flats I lived in as a child, and *Half a Bike* is around here. Roy, the main character, steals a bike from outside the local swimming baths. I went up there to case the joint, to see what bikes were there, and how Roy might go about stealing one.

Summary

Where is your novel set? Familiar locations are helpful in terms of character and plot, and then with marketing opportunities when you have finished the book. You don't have to use a famous place. Or rather, you can make your locale famous with your series.

EXERCISE 5

Imagine you are using your local area as the setting for your crime novel. Write down:

a) 10 places in your area where your main character might go

b) two people who might be in each location. Say what they are doing.

CHAPTER 7: Plot and Main Character

A police procedural could begin with Inspector A coming into the station, some station politics to get some tension going. Inspector A could be in trouble for some unorthodox behaviour, perhaps an internal investigation is underway. We could have that subplot going through the novel. Maybe certain of his colleagues find it difficult to look him in the eye because of what they have said to the investigator. Having introduced Inspector A and some of his colleagues, there's a phone call. There's a body in a house.

Off goes Inspector A, probably with Sergeant B, to the scene. Already there are CSI. Our main characters tog up in crime scene gear and go into the house where CSI are doing their stuff. They interview who lives there and nearby...

And so forth.

One reason police procedurals are so popular is that the police have a job to do when there's a murder. This is the 'procedural' bit, where you need to do research into police activity if you are writing such a novel. Even if you are not going for that type, the cops are going to come into it, and you need to know how they work.

Inspector A is not simply a cop. He has a home life and friends, and these complicate the tale. He could be married with children, or could have an on-off relationship with a girlfriend, who is getting to the end of her tether with his continual cancellations of their dates. Or he might be engaged, with his fiancée having second thoughts at his long hours and the stress he brings along when they do get together.

You need to explore the main characters through their thoughts, actions and their interactions. Don't feel the need to rush to blood and gore with police characters that are only ciphers. I have read books like this, and put them down pretty quickly. It is not simply plot and sensation that holds a reader; we need characters we care about.

How my Jack books work

A typical Jack plot goes something like this:

- Jack goes to a new job (in a house, park, school, cemetery etc)

- He meets the people there as he works and during breaks

- Some romance begins

- A problem with his teenage daughter, via a phone call perhaps

I have to know exactly the work that Jack is doing. In *Jack by the Hedge*, he is working in a park, repairing a wall that has been knocked down by a tractor. I had to research how to build a brick wall. It's all there on YouTube. I am grateful to numerous builders who shared their knowledge via their videos.

You will note in the above plot there is no murder yet. I can't have it too soon as the setting would become a crime scene and Jack wouldn't be able to work while CSI are busy. So with an early murder, he (and the readers) wouldn't get to know the characters in the place. I must hold off until the people in the setting are explored. That doesn't mean there can't be smaller crises, in fact there must be: anger and rows, lies and hatreds coming to the surface. There have to be tensions for there to be a murder, and uncertainty as to who is the perpetrator. Examples in my series are:

- *Jack Recalled*: a brother and sister in the house hate each other, the brother's teenage children are at loggerheads.

- *Jack by the Hedge*: a bully of a foreman is antagonising his workers.

- *Jack of Spades*: a nasty, racist tenant is hated by the others in a large house.

- *Jack in the Box:* anarchists are squatting in a house, to the anger of the households on either side.

- *Jack on the Tower*: an unemployed husband is having an affair with the cleaner while the wife is at work.

Such tensions are vital. We are not playing *Happy Families*. As I have intimated, unlike a police procedural, an early murder presents difficulties for me as Jack would be cleared off the scene. In spite of having a late murder, say halfway through the book, I have to hold my reader. I do this with tensions between characters (rows, fights, unrequited love etc), love interest for Jack, family difficulties for him and so on.

I don't plot out the novel from A to Z. There are writers that do, working out what will happen chapter by chapter through the book. I can't do that. I recall on a school visit, being in a classroom as a visiting writer, with the teacher insisting on a total plan for the children's story. So much of it, that the writer is bored before they get down to the actual writing. Many writers cannot work that way. We have a place, some characters, and off we go, planning as we go along.

Initially for me, the plot is wide open. Someone is going to get killed, sure, but I don't know who. Let's introduce the people, stoke up the tensions and see what I can produce.

I know the work Jack has to do before I start writing, I know the place and the people there vaguely. I get him working, shovelling, drilling and interacting. For quite a few chapters, I am unsure who the victim is going to be. I am keeping my options open as I get deeper in. Then I decide.

In one book, I won't say which as it would be a spoiler, having killed the victim, I had lots of suspects. But I hadn't decided which of them was the murderer. I did something which surprises me to think back on it. I calculatedly, cold bloodedly, said to myself, 'Who is the least likely person to have done it?'

And made them the murderer. I had to make it all tie up by the time Jack works it out in the penultimate chapter. But that's the art of the whodunit. The reader may have rejected someone completely and they turn out to be the killer.

Hey presto!

In Chapter 15, **Plot as You Go**, I show my working plot ladder for *Jack on the Tower*. Here it is in summary. I finish writing a chapter and in my ladder write in a line or so about what has happened. Then I write a heading, 'Next', and jot down where I think I'll be going. I might change my mind as I get further in or stick with what I've got if it's working. When I've done another chapter, I'll continue the ladder and add more to Next.

Making a Main Character

You need a description of him or her. Not that detailed, as who remembers book descriptions unless a characteristic is exceptional? Like being very short, very tall, a great beauty, having a long shaggy beard, or being completely bald. Jack has none of these. Lord Peter Wimsey has a cane and monocle, which are very distinctive and aristocratic, but I can't recall how tall he is, what colour his hair is or his eyes. I know he dresses well and expensively, and Bunter, 'his man', is there to make sure of this. Sherlock Holmes we recall with the magnifying glass and deerstalker. Tall, I think, though am I confusing him with his many screen avatars?

A main character, especially for a series, must be sympathetic. Not perfect, that's boring, but we should care about them. Ripley, Patricia Highsmith's serial killer, is on the margins here. It's impossible to warm to this parasitical killer, though Highsmith does try to mute his nasty side. This didn't work for me. And I've only read the first in the five book series.

In films, villains such as Hannibal Lecter (from Thomas Harris' series) can be contrasted with his antagonist, played by Jodie Foster in the movies. She is an FBI agent, and stands for civility and shares our nausea of Lecter. In *Silence of the Lambs* Lecter won the accolades but I certainly couldn't stomach much more of this freak who eats the flesh of his victims. Making him cultured didn't work for me, and I wasn't surprised that the other Hannibal Lecter films didn't do nearly as well.

Lecter is a variation on *Dr Jekyll and Mr Hyde*, Robert Louis Stevenson's classic novel. Dr Jekyll is a respectable doctor, who transforms into Hyde, a killer, by drinking a serum. Lecter needs no serum. There are two sides to him, the socialite of impeccable taste, fooling everyone until we see the psychopath in him.

Note that Stevenson didn't attempt a sequel. My contention is that psychopaths as a main character work well once, as there are plenty of surprises before the reveal. Once we know what we are getting, we are less keen on them. And the readership drops for subsequent novels.

Questions to Answer

You need to know your main character well. Here's some questions you should be able to answer:

- What do they do for a living?
- What skills do they have?
- Income (well off, getting by, struggling)?
- Where do they live (town, type of dwelling)?
- What are their main relationships?
- What do other people think of them?
- What are their hobbies?
- Do they have a spouse or partner?
- Any children?
- Characteristics (grumpy, a sense of humour, clever, talkative, likeable)?
- Some back history (parents, education, prior employment, marriage etc. Don't go to town on this.)
- Weaknesses (drink, drugs, sexual cheating, put upon, moaning)

You won't know all this at the beginning. You will learn more as you write the first draft. Through their relationships, and what they do. And some of the above may well change. If you are writing a series then you will know more with each book.

Certain aspects will require research. That could include your main character's job. They may have employment other than sleuthing, as I do with my builder, Jack. Whether this is farming, baking, accountancy, or taxi driving, you will need to know something about their work. Such research always pays off by making your character more believable.

Your character may be religious, with a religion other than your own. Research it. You could give them your own hobby, say, if it's gardening, crosswords, chess or playing in a blues band. Other than that, research it.

If your main character is a cop, chapters 19 and 20 will assist. Even if not, all crime writers need to know how the police work as inevitably a murder will involve them. For a police procedural, the writer must know their protagonist's rank, their department, who they work with and how they work on a murder investigation. As well as their home life and other activities beyond their job.

My Main Character

He is Jack Bell, a simple name, an everyman. I originally had his surname as Spencer, but sometimes I would spell it Spenser and sometimes Spencer. I got quite befuddled, and thought this is no good, I need a surname with only one spelling. So, Bell.

Now there are nine books (and another in the wings), I know a lot about Jack. Not everything by any means. I will drop the odd bit of his history in from time to time, and hopefully not forget it. But you don't need it all to begin with. Just so much for your first story, and then add more as you need it. Your main character will develop through their interaction with other people. Jack reads the Daily Mirror and has a regular monthly astronomy magazine. They have come up. Lots hasn't.

I have never given his exact age. He is mid to late 30s. I wanted some flexibility on this. But he has a daughter, 10 years old in the first book, 14 in the latest. She is the signaller of time passing. Ian Rankin's Inspector Rebus ages throughout the series. In the first novel he's 40 and in the last novels he's in his 60s.

You don't have to age your character. I could keep him at 35, and he could have a 10 year old daughter for as long as I keep writing about him. Though having decided to age his daughter, I have forgone this option. But I do have the option to freeze him at a particular age. Or even go back in time, though that might confuse the reader.

Lynda La Plante goes back in time with her main character, Jane Tennison. We know her first as a Detective Chief Inspector in *Prime Suspect* when she is middle aged. Recently, La Plante has given us the same character as a 22 year old rookie. But with at least 30 years' difference in age, and many steps down in the hierarchy, there's no confusion.

Sherlock Holmes doesn't seem to age until the end when he retires to the Sussex Downs and keeps bees. By giving him no children, Conan Doyle could have him almost static.

Jack is a builder, his main skill is carpentry but he has picked up other building skills. He can do some bricklaying, some roofing, lay paving, concreting. He mostly works alone. He calls his one-man firm Jack of All Trades. The name is on his van. It is regularly commented on. 'And master of none,' he has heard too many times. His practised rejoinder is, 'At least you'll remember me.'

Initially, I thought I'd make him somewhat sloppy in his trade, having troubles with customers. But I dropped this and have made him a good worker, though he still has troubles with customers, making an uneasy living, often in debt. Some of this may be due to the murders on site, when he doesn't get paid.

He was married to Alison, who kept her married name Bell after their divorce, as she is a primary school teacher and her daughter is Mia Bell. She kicked Jack out for alcoholism, and he spent several weeks on the streets before giving up drink, though he relapses when I need him to.

He and Mia get on well most of the time. She stays every other weekend, but other evenings too when Alison is working late or is on a date. Mia and Jack often go out with his telescope onto Wanstead Flats to view the stars. She knows as much as he does.

He and Alison sometimes argue and other times call a truce, though they'd have little to do with each other if they weren't Mia's parents. Alison in the first book is a senior teacher and in the latter books she is the school principal. Jack remains a struggling builder. He goes to Alcohol Halt from time to time, an organisation for alcoholics in recovery. He has a mentor, Max, who he sometimes asks for advice.

Jack is not well educated. He messed around in the last few years in secondary school, bunked off too often, and so left with few qualifications. But building has taught him a lot. There's no one to fall back on. He must assess a job, price it, buy materials, have the skills to do it, deal with customers and any problems that come up, and do his own accounts. His hobby of astronomy has taught him quite a bit too. He reads the magazine assiduously, will get books from the library. And Mia keeps him up to scratch.

He is sharp, which is not the same as being well educated as you can have all the degrees and be quite stupid. He is analytical. Much of that comes from his building sense. Buildings are logical. You can see what is holding them up or follow a pipe to find out where it is leaking. A builder is expected to know the answers. Where he doesn't, Jack will go online and seek out the answers for both building problems and his sleuthing.

Jack has a friend, Bob, who he sees less often now that he is not drinking, but Bob does get him work from time to time and helps out with equipment. Jack can also turn to him if he has a building problem.

I suspect I have made mistakes in my chronology but no reader has come back at me. Most don't notice any slight contradiction, and if they do, don't care. He has been 5 feet

9 or 10 and has brown curly hair. And mostly wears overalls when working. This is definitely a throwback to my father, who wore navy blue, bibbed overalls when he worked.

He has girlfriend trouble in each book, and never has the same one from book to book. I decided to keep him single, which allows me a love angle as a sub plot, and keeps him a bit unhappy. Some of his girlfriends are murdered, some are murderers. Of course, I never know this at the beginning of the book. It happens.

EXERCISE 6

Take a character of yours and interview them. This is a useful technique for finding out more about them, akin to the way actors work in exploring a character.

If you don't have a character, then interview the baddy in a fairy story, say the wolf or the giant. A baddy will not likely admit they are bad. They will lie to you. Alternatively, they could boast of their wickedness.

CHAPTER 8: Sidekicks and Other Characters

One of the best known crime-fighting duos is Batman and Robin. Batman is rather like Lord Peter Wimsey. When not being Batman, he is the socialite Bruce Wayne, owning a large, gothic house and having a butler, and other servants too who mostly stay below stairs. Robin is his ward Dick Grayson, and, when the dynamic duo surface, his sidekick in crime fighting.

Originally they were DC comic heroes, but now are much better known through films. I'd regard them as amateur private eyes, like Lord Peter Wimsey, but closely allied to the police. They are called up by the Bat-Signal, beamed by Police Commissioner Gordon over the skies of Gotham City, to alert them to another serious crime. It has its ridiculous elements which is why it is played tongue in cheek in movies. How can they not be recognised in those half masks, how can they not be tracked back to the Batcave, why don't the baddies simply shoot them?

They are superheroes, but without superpowers, and yet they beat the Joker, Cat Woman, and the Penguin. The pair don't really stand a chance being only human. But they win out. It's a fairy story for all the family.

Robin is Batman's sidekick. The sidekick can be of inferior status, like Robin, or an equal. Becoming equal is another Robin, Cormoran Strike's assistant at first and then partner, to her fiancé's chagrin. A bugbear of mine, in the

TV series, is that she wears high heels. And of course, has to take them off to run. Not recommended wear for a private eye.

We have equals in the partnerships of Cagney and Lacey, two New York City cops in the 1980s TV series. It was groundbreaking stuff, giving two female cops such prominence, shooting and fighting as well as their male colleagues. And balancing home lives with police shifts too.

One can scarcely think about sidekicks without conjuring up Dr Watson (with his faithful service revolver). Watson is the narrator of the Sherlock Holmes tales and usually misreads the clues. How many innocents would be rotting in jail if it were left to Watson? Or, I might add, Inspector Lestrade, a bumbling Scotland Yard cop, who Holmes always has to put right.

The sidekick is someone the main character can talk to, explain their reasoning, argue with. It can be like a marriage, with good days and bad days, sulks and tantrums. Poor Sergeant Lewis has to put up with the cantankerous Inspector Morse, in Colin Dexter's books. Lewis is inferior in rank, but does argue back, though ultimately Morse can pull rank. Lewis and Morse are contrasted in their education and choices of entertainment. Morse has an Oxford degree and delights in opera and classical music while his sergeant watches soaps and listens to pop music. After Morse's death, Lewis became the lead in the eponymous TV series, having learnt a lot from his mentor.

Is Bunter the sidekick of Lord Peter Wimsey (in Dorothy L Sayers' novels)? Sometimes referred to as 'my man' by Wimsey, they were in WWI together, Bunter being his batman. Bunter cooks and cleans, runs errands, and does the odd bit of detective work. His photography and dark-room skills are vital in the investigations. But I'd say he isn't really a sidekick. Bunter is too inferior in class and by class rules, Wimsey's confidant has to be someone nearer his rank. Can you really have a sidekick who refers to his partner as 'my lord'? So we have Charles Parker, at first a detective sergeant at Scotland Yard, but he rises in rank throughout the series to Commissioner Parker, and marries Wimsey's sister Mary.

Parker and Wimsey often eat together. If at home, the meal is served by Bunter. In later books, Harriet Vane, a writer of crime mysteries, becomes his detective partner. And in the end, his wife.

Lawrence Block's Bernie Rhodenbarr, the bookseller and burglar has as confidante Carolyn Kaiser. She is a lesbian, so no sexual hassles. He tells her what he is up to and discusses possibilities in their cultured tête-à-têtes.

Elly Griffiths has Detective Inspector Edgar Stephens and Max Mephisto the stage magician as partners in her early 1950s Brighton novels. They were in a special operations team during the war. Griffiths has her work cut out bringing them together, as Stephens has plenty of work as a cop and Max Mephisto is a busy illusionist. It's a good pairing with the cop having the resources of the police force, but needing the insights of the illusionist.

Jack Bell's sidekicks

Initially, I used the women in Jack's life as confidantes. But this is not the best of modes, as those relationships break up, and some get murdered, and some are murderers. In the latter case, it can prove harmful to your health giving them your thoughts on the crime.

From *Jack on the Tower* onwards, Detective Sergeant Fayyad Kamani might be regarded as his sidekick. Jack and he work closely on a number of cases. Not that Jack can be completely open with Fayyad, as he has a guilty secret which, if it came out, would result in a jail sentence.

Fayyad and Jack are the same age. They were at school together. Jack was in the school football team while Fayyad is a good cricketer. He now plays for the police. His boss, Detective Superintendent Nikki Martin, is a cricket umpire, and so favours Fayyad. Fayyad is married and lives in Ilford, about 2 miles from Forest Gate, and has two children. He is a Muslim, his parents are Pakistani. Jack has visited him in Ilford several times, but these are only referred to. We haven't yet met the family. Fayyad is a smart dresser, always wearing a suit and tie. He prides himself in looking the part.

As the series went on, I needed Jack to have a pal in the police so he can keep up with the police investigation, especially forensic information: fingerprinting, DNA, the autopsy etc. Fayyad drops in to see Jack to express his concerns. I have no doubt he is telling Jack too much about the case, and would be in trouble if his superiors knew. But Jack is wise enough to keep quiet.

So Fayyad functions as a friend, someone to discuss the case with, but there is also an edge of tension, as Fayyad is still a cop, and Jack has stepped over the line.

Family and Other Characters

Characters are not Ben Gunn, alone on Treasure Island, abandoned by the pirates and dreaming of cheese. They exist in a nexus of people. Sartre said that we only exist in the eyes of other people. You are a parent, a sibling, a grandparent because others treat you that way. If suddenly they denied who you were, mentally you'd be in big trouble.

There has to be someone to be kind to, to hate, or to love. We live in a world of people. Alone we disintegrate.

Jack is a father, a builder, a friend, a lover because of the way other people behave towards him. A plot theme, used a number of times, is when someone comes home – and no one knows them. This happens to James Stewart in the 1946 film *It's a Wonderful Life*. And he is bewildered, horrified.

There is no one to affirm his existence, he is nullified. Fortunately, an angel changes things to the way they were.

While affirmation happens all the time, it isn't always good. Sartre also said, Hell is other people. That hell could emanate from your boss, your colleagues, your neighbours, your brother, your child, your spouse. And drive you to murder.

Motive

Why might A want to kill B? Phrased another way: what motive have they? A question always asked when the police (or reader) are considering who the suspects are for the murder. For a whodunit we need a number of suspects to keep our reader puzzling. Even if the reader knows who did it, we don't want the police going straight to the murderer, or you'll have a very short, and unsatisfying book.

The main motives for murder are money, property, jealousy, revenge, racism, nationalism and religion. No shortage. These can of course double up. A brother might be jealous of his younger brother's financial success or his girlfriend, or both. Revenge can be for something recent, when a boss fires a worker for example, or could go back many years when a woman believes someone killed her father, and has tracked them down over decades. 'Honour killing' is a type of revenge, when a daughter marries out of her religion and her siblings vow to kill her for 'disgracing' the family. Racism is often random in that a man or woman is killed simply because they were the wrong colour and encountered a racist gang.

None of this is pleasant. Murder never is, bringing out the worst aspects of human nature. But this nature is part of their character, which the individual will try to hide, but will be revealed in the end. Perhaps piecemeal, by a hint in the way they treat a pet or a child.

Families

We come back, time and time again, to family. Do happy families exist? It depends when you ask. It depends who you ask. A father might believe his family is a happy one, his wife may agree in his company, but feel otherwise. There's no need to go further down this road, as we are not interested in happy families even if they do exist. It's unhappy ones that give us the scope we need as crime writers. We want animosity to give us motives and suspects.

Family feuds: our fiction and history return to them all the time.

Much of the Wars of the Roses was a family saga, members of the same family fighting to briefly take the crown. Elizabeth I imprisoned her cousin Mary Queen of Scots, and finally executed her for treason. The reason these stories appeal to us is because we all have families. On our smaller stage, we recognise the fierce emotions that can build up in the family.

In my *Jack o'Lantern* we have two sisters who hate each other. In *Jack Recalled,* ditto: a brother and sister. In *Jack at Death's Door*, a family are quarrelling to control a cemetery. Such enmity is the stock in trade of the crime novelist. Create your family and ensure it has antagonisms.

A friend of mine had his family torn apart by his widowed mother's will. She left the house to the youngest son. A son who had a good job and was single. He had no need for the house, while another son had a family with young children and was badly housed and in an insecure job. A sister had been looking after the mother in the last year of her life. She did well out of the will. How much influence had she had on the making of the will? Ask any member of the family and you'll get different answers.

It wasn't the butler. It was the spouse/the son/the sister.

Description of Minor Characters

We don't remember descriptions unless there's something unusual about them. You could pick on one unusual visual aspect.

Taking off his beret, Jack could see he was utterly bald, his dome catching the light as if painted in pink gloss.

She was seventy if she was a day, and had a wild bush of hair as bright as a sunset.

Both of these are strikingly visual. We can see them. How much more do we need? It depends on whether they are recurring characters or encountered only once.

EXERCISE 7

Invent a family, with two parents and three grown up siblings. Give them names. The parents own a restaurant and call a meeting as they want to retire. What are the siblings' attitudes to the retirement, who sides with whom?

CHAPTER 9:
Description of Place and Characters

In our crime novel, we need to describe places and people, so that our reader can imagine them. A description of a place can be pure and disembodied, but you need to be a superb stylist to attempt that. Rather, you can see the place through your character's eyes. That way you are doing two things at once, seeing the place and learning more about the character seeing it.

This piece from near the beginning of *Jack by the Hedge* illustrates what I mean.

```
The street lights suddenly went off.
Officially day. In the sky were slow
moving white clouds in large patches of
blue. To the east, the orange-yellow wash
of dawn, a low sun hidden behind the roof
tops. There was a slight breeze, not a
bad working temperature. With luck, it
wouldn't rain today and he could get well
into the job. With all that clear sky,
maybe tonight he could get out with his
telescope.
     Jack looked at his watch. Seven thirty,
the man had said, and seven thirty it was
```

now. And there he was unlocking the gate from the inside. An early start, and here they both were. Jack lifted the wheelbarrow handles and pushed the barrow the twenty metres to the gate.

The man was swinging back the wide ironwork gate, wide enough to take a lorry, ornate scrolling above the vertical bars, almost gothic in grandeur, as if there were a stately home behind it and not a public park in Plaistow. The man was locking the gate in its open position and, it seemed to Jack, he was deliberately ignoring him, waiting with his wheelbarrow.

Jack knew his sort.

He was sure this was the same person he'd spoken to on the phone on Friday. An officious sod, dressed to kill any doubt, in a brown suit with a matching waistcoat, brown leather shoes, highly polished, and brown hair, too brown. A man with so well-used a face would have grey in his hair. The nose was flattened, as if for the first few years someone had sat on it.

In the first paragraph, we have dawn and plenty of blue sky, and Jack hoping it stays clear for the evening so he can be out with his telescope. With his wheelbarrow, Jack goes to the gate, and there he is ignored as the man opens the gate, someone Jack has spoken to on the phone and Jack's description of him brings out his dislike. We also know who is above whom in the hierarchy: the man in the suit and the man with the wheelbarrow.

We have immediate tension between Jack and the man opening the gate in the first few paragraphs of the book. His description of him is less than flattering. Imagine the same person being described by an equal who really liked him. The hair dye could be seen as a symbol of a man keen to stay young, his flattened nose signifying experience.

Consider how our attitudes to people change. A man may consider his fiancée the most beautiful woman in the world. Ten years later, after their divorce, he finds her grotesque. Neither attitude is objective of course, both tempered by need. If we described her through his eyes, first as his fiancée and then as his ex wife, we would hardly know her to be the same person.

At the beginning of the next chapter of *Jack by the Hedge*, a new character is introduced. The reader has not met her before. As you read this extract, consider how much we are learning about her through the description of what she sees.

In 2 Balaam Cottages, one of the two park houses, Liz was at the table in the kitchen spooning muesli and banana. The weekend had been a good one. She'd seen her parents on Saturday, then yesterday been out with her painting group over Hampstead Heath. She'd had a number of goes at capturing leaves floating on a pond in watercolours, and one had worked well, caught the bronze and yellows, the reflections of cloud and trees and the tinges of death. The others she'd torn up.

She gazed out of the window, at the sky and trees. There was still an orange edge to the day. Difficult to catch in paint, the sun up and unsure, shadows longish, dawn oozing away through the half bare, autumn trees.

Or should she photograph it and work from that? But that always felt a cheat,

second hand. If you are going to photograph then photograph - and leave it
there. Paint from the original. She could
surprise herself in her puritanism.

Friday, she'd found some death stalk
mushrooms in the shrubbery. She'd like to
paint them growing out of the leaf mould.
So ordinary looking, the white stalk, the
umbrella top with a touch of yellow-
green. So delicate, so deadly, surrounded
by the empty husks of beech nuts. She'd
picked a couple and had them in a display
on her sideboard on a sheet of pale
yellow card amid leaves of red, yellow
and crinkled brown, with purple sloes,
chestnuts, ash twigs with their black,
match-head buds.

Liz wasn't sentimental about nature.
Everything died in the end. That didn't
kill the beauty of the season. Maybe
added to it, the temporariness of things.
Everything has its day. She couldn't help
but glance in the mirror. No grey hairs
yet in her red hair, her freckles were
fading again. She looked her years, mid
30s. Her sister though looked maybe five
years younger than her actual age.

We learn a lot in these few paragraphs. We know it is
autumn and Liz lives in one of the cottages in the park and
is a painter. This is the reader's introduction to her. I could
have said more in the piece, but chose not to. Storytelling is
about making the reader curious, wanting to know more. All
in good time.

She is seeing the same sky as Jack. He sees it as a man
with a telescope, she as a painter. We learn about her love of
beauty, without sentimentality, and her puritanism. Always

a dangerous attribute. She looks in a mirror and we get a brief description of her. On her sideboard, she has an autumn display of leaves, buds and mushrooms. The mushrooms are poisonous, and I am slipping them in quietly, amidst the colours and seeds. They will be the instrument of murder.

Bear In Mind

Do two things at once with descriptions of places. Have a character seeing it through their eyes. So you have character as well as the place in your description. Your story will be the richer for it.

EXERCISE 8

Write a single visual aspect for each of two characters. Make it striking.

CHAPTER 10:

Monologue or Dialogue?

A monologue is when one person is speaking. It may be a character telling another (and the reader) about their past life, their relationships, their fears etc, in a long piece with minimal interruption. It might be at the end of the novel as in classic Agatha Christie, when Poirot has all the suspects in the drawing room, and explains everything in detail. He is rarely interrupted as he goes through the clues and suspects one by one.

This should be pure storytelling, holding the reader by their curiosity. There are similarities with the soliloquy in the theatre but there is a major difference. Hamlet in his soliloquy 'To be or not to be' is telling the audience about his thoughts on suicide. In a novel, these thoughts would not be spoken as the writer can tell us what someone is thinking.

Though not quite everyone. We'll come back to this with point of view in a later chapter.

We are looking at spoken monologue here, not thoughts. One person speaking. If you are using this, for back story, say, you must keep it interesting or your reader will skip it. And if they've done it once, it is easier to do it a second time, and you may have lost a reader.

The monologue has to be a story in itself, with a beginning, middle and end. With tension and all the tricks of storytelling.

This paragraph is from *Jack of Spades*. Anne, a childminder, and Jack are having dinner. Jack has a few one line interjections but it is mostly Anne speaking about the murder of her husband (Malcolm). CPS is the Crime Prosecution Service, who decide in the UK whether there is enough evidence for a case to go for trial.

'The CPS had a tight case, circumstan-
tial. And lies from a couple of
witnesses. Well, I was having an affair
to make it worse. The upshot was I was
found guilty. And spent two years in the
nick. Horrible, horrible time. Then they
found out who actually did it. And I was
freed.'

'How long ago was this?'

'I've been out for three years,' she
said. 'Once I was free, I got Malcolm's
life insurance and the money for his
flat. I didn't want to stick around in
Manchester. Too many people had said
nasty things about me. I wanted a fresh
start. So came down to London. Bought
this flat and spent a year trying to get
a job. It does make the mess of a CV, two
years in jail. Even telling lies about it
means you have to tell more to fill in
what you were doing in the time. In the
end I thought, I have a bit of money,
what can I do? And came up with child-
minding. I did a course, got the nursery
set up, went through the inspection…' She
bit her thumb. 'I was so thoroughly
inspected. That prison spell stumped them
for a bit, till I went to a solicitor,

73

and they caved in. Got my first children
six months ago. And here I am. Ex jail-
bird makes good.'

A monologue, with a single interjection from Jack. Plenty
there to get the reader asking questions. Does Jack believe
her? Does the reader? It's uncertainty that makes us want to
read on.

Dialogue

Dialogue is two or more people talking. Strictly two, but we
use the same word for several characters involved in a
conversation. It has a number of functions in a novel. Some
of which may be working at the same time. Dialogue is vital
in a crime story, from police questioning to a row between
husband and wife. It can move a plot quickly. A character
may reveal something, suggest a course of action, or tell a
character exactly what to do.

A whole story can be told in a dialogue. Take a play.
There's visuals too, but a radio play is speech, a few sound
effects and music. Actors can be very expressive with their
voices of course, so a radio play isn't simply words, but it's
pretty close, showing how much dialogue can do.

So much.

Dialogue can give information about other characters or
about a situation. A character can be asked something
directly (but of course they may be lying, for any number of
reasons. Perhaps to protect someone, or themselves.) Misin-
formation (i.e. a lie) may be an important part of the plot.

We can use dialogue to bring the reader up to date; to
say what was happening before the story started or in
another place. Beware though, too much information can
kill tension.

Dialogue shows how relationships are working. Characters may argue, shout at each other, make friends or cease to be friends. Relationships change, shift back and forth, sometimes permanently, sometimes just for a time. Or can make permanent enmity, fermenting a brew of revenge.

Aspects of character come out in dialogue. We speak differently to different people. Compare someone speaking to a friend, to the same person speaking to a policeman, or a film star they are a fan of. In the latter case, they may be speechless, voluble with a friend, ultra careful with a cop. If we want them less careful, we as *deus ex machina* can get them drunk. Or engender a sexual encounter, with emotions high.

Though sex often occasions lies. A married man with two children wants to keep that dark. A practised liar perhaps. Some people are superb at it. Actors do it for a living (and writers too).

The same character may be confident, shy, intelligent, stupid, happy, sad - all of which will be revealed in their speech, depending on who they are talking to. They may be talkative or taciturn, have a regional accent or speak 'posh'. Class is an important part of character, believing ourselves superior or inferior.

Dialogue can add humour. The stuff of sitcoms. Funny situations or repartee, the art of insults. It adds variety to storytelling, breaking up chunks of narration.

Silence and Evasion

Sometimes not answering a question can be more important than answering it. A character may be silent or may evade the question, the way that politicians do. The reader then knows something isn't right but doesn't know what. Fine: one of your aims as a writer is to keep your reader curious, and reveal exactly what in your own good time.

In the interview room at the police station, a suspect may keep silent or say 'no comment' to every question. Judge that how you will.

Body Language

Dialogue in a book is not the same as dialogue in a play. In the play the actors give speech life. In a book you have to. Think of what characters are doing when they are speaking. Our faces and bodies express our emotions too. Note the following:

- 'Give me that book,' he said, teeth gritted and fists up.

- 'Give me that book,' he said, keeping his distance, one arm stretched out feebly.

The first character is determined to get the book, and will fight for it. The second has given it up already. Body language helps the reader to see the characters as they speak.

In this example of dialogue taken from *Jack by the Hedge*, we have a sexual encounter. We have met both characters before. They are Jack, the builder and Liz who lives in a house in the park. Jack is working on a wall that has been hit by a tractor. He is knocking out the dislodged bricks. Later he will replace them. There is a mention of Rose who is Liz's sister, and was recently staying with Liz.

```
Liz had crossed the main lawn and was
nearing the bowling green, where the
builder was knocking at the mortar
between the bricks with a hammer and
```

chisel. He was wearing a yellow hard hat and safety goggles.

'Lovely morning,' he called, raising his hat slightly.

'Beautiful,' said Liz. 'We haven't had a frost yet, though I like the sharpness.' She looked over his work. 'Are you going to put the old bricks back?'

'I've been thinking about that,' said Jack. 'The bricks in the yard are the wrong colour.'

'Most of those could be reused,' she said, indicating the bricks he'd knocked out.

Jack picked up a brick and shook his head. 'It would take me ages to knock the mortar off all of them.'

'But it would look so much better,' she insisted.

He nodded. 'It would. But the manager wants…'

'Knocking on the head,' she interrupted with a laugh, 'with that hammer.'

Jack smiled. A long smile that faded into the intensity of his stare.

She held the look, thinking: Oh. His eyes, the curl of hair sticking out of the helmet, his hands on the hammer and chisel. A hit out of nowhere. She wasn't used to this. Not for a long time. Had Rose made her vulnerable?

'Do you work here?' he said at last, without looking away.

'Yes,' she was able to manage. 'There.' She pointed, her arm still able to move. 'In the greenhouses.'

Neither spoke for a few seconds, eyes liquid light. In slow motion, he put the hammer onto the top of the wall.

She said hesitantly, 'You can come over when I open up. No, come for a tea break. Ten thirty.' She took a couple of steps away and gave him a shy wave. 'I really must go, the manager gets shirty if anyone's late.'

'I've met the creep,' he said, almost normally. 'See you for tea.'

She turned away, crossed the drive and went into the yard, her stomach swirling like a roll of tumbleweed.

There's lots of body language, which says as much as words. Eyes, silence, a shy wave. Note that it is written from her point of view. We know her thoughts directly, his only indirectly from what he says and his body language.

A relationship is being established, and moved on a step as she has invited Jack to her greenhouse during the tea break. This is a subplot of the novel. There hasn't been a murder yet. I have things to set up beforehand.

We have information about the work Jack is doing, and how the bricks he has been given to repair the wall don't match the extant piece of wall. Will Jack tell the manager this? We know he doesn't like him (and neither does Liz).

Several things are brought out through this dialogue which is why it holds us. And makes us curious about what is going to happen between Jack and Liz, and Jack and the manager.

He said, she said

Make it clear who is speaking in your dialogue. It is annoying to lose track and then have to count back. I have had to do it too often in novels I've read. The writer has ripped the dialogue away from the speaker. There's just dialogue, as if we are there, watching as it is spoken. But we are not there to see whose lips are moving.

Don't annoy your reader by having them lose track who is speaking. Put in sufficient 'he saids/she saids'. They won't spoil your style; the reader will hardly notice them.

Use Dialogue for Your Purpose

Dialogue is not simply chatter. It is not like listening in on a conversation on a bus. Dialogue in a book has aims: it can further the plot, tell us more about characters and relationships, or discuss what is happening. You decide what is said.

Dialogue in a novel may resemble real life dialogue, but is in fact far more purposeful. In good dialogue, readers shouldn't notice this. They are too involved.

Like description, with dialogue you should try to do *at least two things at once*. Give information, say, and move a relationship. Where a dialogue does just one then the reader will see it as thin.

EXERCISE 9

Reread the dialogue in this chapter between Jack and Liz. Imagine you are in the park going for a stroll. It is autumn, leaves falling.

Write in first person as yourself. Have a chat with Jack about the work he is doing, rebuilding the wall. Then go to the greenhouse and have a chat with Liz. Just a few minutes with them; they are working, you're not.

CHAPTER 11: Point of View

I was a playwright for twelve years or so, and had 21 plays performed, some co-written. When I attempted to write a novel in the early 80s, I made a complete hash of it. There are things plays don't have, like description. Well, I knew that. It's obvious. There's also thought, although it can be delivered in a soliloquy, but it's not the same as thought in a book. As noted in the last chapter, a soliloquy is a chunk of thought, rather than on-going thought. I understood that.

But there were things I didn't know I didn't know.

That first novel was a mishmash. There were good bits, there were awful bits. I couldn't make it fit. I didn't know what I was doing.

So I went to an evening class on writing fiction at the City Lit, in Holborn, central London. I skipped the beginners' class. Well, I'd had all those plays performed, I was no beginner. I'd also missed the first term. Well, I'd pick it up. I was both absolutely confident and not confident at all. But I was open, having got to the point of knowing I didn't know how to write a novel.

In the class, I found at once a new vocabulary. 'Point of view' kept coming up. I had no idea what this was. You don't need it for a play. As a playwright, you move your characters on and off stage, as if they are puppets. You decide on their entrances and exits.

I couldn't get to grips with point of view in the class. They'd done that first term and so were tossing the phrase about as if everybody knew what it was. One student didn't. So I read up on it, and it began to filter in. Point of view is whose eyes and head you are choosing to see a scene from. Well, that hit me. How had I missed it? It was in every bit of fiction I read.

Let's get our heads round it.

There are three common points of view:

- First Person

- Third Person

- Omniscient Narrator

First person is 'I'. You are being talked to directly by a character in the novel. Sometimes a main character as in Dickens' *Great Expectations* where Pip is telling us his tale. Or *Catcher in the Rye*, J D Salinger's novel with Holden Caulfield narrating. Such novels can be very direct and powerful. Someone is talking to you specifically. We like that. It's flattering, even if it's an illusion. Watson, Sherlock Holmes' sidekick, is the first person narrator of the tales. He tells us what he sees and knows. At times, Holmes disappears and Watson has no idea what he is up to, until Holmes reappears and tells him.

A point to clear up before we go further. Point of view and viewpoint character are essentially the same thing. We might say:

- *Jack is the viewpoint character in chapter one.*

- Or *chapter one is written from Jack's point of view.*

My first novel, written for young adults, *Hard Cash*, is told in the first person. We could rephrase that as written from first person point of view, or told from the viewpoint of Shorty, a 13 year old boy. Here are the beginning paragraphs. It is allowable for me to use them as an example, as it is a crime story. Faber told me so.

Warby asked me to write it down. He said I was the one who was good at that sort of thing and he was sick of people saying things that just weren't true. As for me - I just want to get it out. There's a lot of talk anyway - so they might as well hear how it was rather than a load of lies.

I've been saying all that because I'm trying to work out where to begin. How much you want to know. Whether I should say what we look like and describe our houses and things. Though I'm not much good at describing things and it'll prob- ably bore you as much reading it as it will bore me writing it.

Myself I like adventure; especially space stories - strange planets and far galaxies. I like it to move so that you can't put it down, you want to know so badly what happens next.

So I'd better jump in. I'll fill in the other bits as we get to them. There was this derelict building on Crisp Street. It wasn't the only derelict building - there were half a dozen of them in a row, all tinned up. Doors, windows - no glass, just corrugated iron. The yards were full of rubbish. Old armchairs, black bags full of rotting rubbish, mattresses, a broken washing machine. You know the sort of stuff that gets dumped.

        This house had the corrugated iron over
the door loose. Not very loose, a bit
loose. And then Warby encouraged it. He's
never one to hold back and he can be a
bit silly. Like when he made faces at
those big kids and got himself beat up.
Dancing up and down, 'Can't catch me'.
Well they could alright and they did
alright. You'd think maybe he would learn
but I don't think he ever will.

There's no hanging about here, straight into the story. Shorty is talking directly to the reader, wondering how to tell the tale. As I was too, as I certainly didn't have it planned. They call this 'seat of the pants' writing. You just keep going, until you get stuck in a cul de sac, or manage to get to the end (to your relief).

It worked for me. I had a voice. Here was a teenager, not very confident, about to go into a derelict building. All sorts of things can be found in derelict buildings. In this instance, they find a quarter of a million pounds in the cellar.

Whatever viewpoint you use, you are telling a story to someone. For me, it goes something like this. First of all, I am telling the tale to myself. But that's not enough. In fact, if it's just to myself it will be quite a poor piece as I won't need to explain all sorts of things. I imagine another reader, not me. I don't know who they are. They are not embodied, I don't know their sex or age. It's like a mental thing, brain to brain. A story has to be told to someone in order to work for everyone.

Especially with first person, you need to get the voice of the character you are pretending to be. You don't want your reader, as if at a party, stifling a yawn, looking over their shoulder for someone to rescue them from this bore.

This book is written in the first person. The major difference is that this is not a novel, and I am not pretending to be someone else. But as I write, beyond writing for me, I am imagining you, my reader. I am talking to you in my head. Fiction is no different in that respect. Writers want to communicate, or what's the point?

Hard Cash was read on BBC radio by Tony Robinson (now Sir Tony) in ten episodes. It was shortlisted for a Sony award, the big prize for radio in the UK. First person is great for an actor when it works. He has a character to get to grips with, and once they have it, the story can come over powerfully.

It was a relief to me, after the mishmash of my first go, that this one worked. I could write, having learned some rules.

Limitations of First Person

First person viewpoint has the strength of directness, but has the weakness of being limited to what the narrator sees. They can tell you what has been going on elsewhere, but only from what other characters tell them. This can get rather contrived.

A way out of this is to have a number of first person characters. So one will tell the story for a chapter, say, and then another will take it on. In my second book to be published, *Frances Fairweather Demon Striker!*, I began it as first person from Frances' point of view. She is a girl football player in trouble at school because all she wants to do is play football. About 70 pages in, I found I had to get away from her. The plot necessitated it. So I made her best friend, Anne, a first person narrator too. This second voice comes over as a surprise, and for a paragraph or two you don't know where you are. And then you realise it is another character talking.

If I were to rewrite the novel, I would introduce Anne as a first person character early on, so the reader would not be hit 70 pages in.

Third Person Viewpoint

This is when we use he or she. Here's another few paragraphs from *Jack by the Hedge* in third person:

It was a pity that switching the bowling green was so speedy. Zar savoured the lash of it, the wide sweep of the glass fibre rod, the drops flying in the air, sparkling in the sunlight, dropping tingling cold on his neck and face. Best not tell Ian he liked it or he'd have him off it and sweeping paths.

He'd like to switch a golf course, walk the whole 18 holes on a misty autumn morning, switching each of the greens from 1 to 18 before the first golfers. Alone, without expectations from anyone.

It was why he liked working in the open air. Space, plants, distance from people. He'd spent a month in his uncle's accountancy office - and hated it. In a dark suit, stuck in front of a screen all day, his uncle trying to impress him with the good money qualified accountants earned, how he could get a big house and garden, have a wife and family. Be secure for the rest of his life, a respected member of the community.

He did not say - but uncle, I am gay. That wasn't a Muslim thing to say. Not to an uncle who was on the committee of the mosque. Or to anyone in his family when

it came to that. Or to anyone in their
circle. There was already talk of finding
him a wife, but he was only twenty,
plenty of time his father said. Pass your
accountancy exams, Zar - and they'll all
want you. You could take your pick.

The book has five different third person viewpoints. The viewpoint characters in the first chapters are:

- Chapter 1, Jack
- Chapter 2, Liz (the painter, who works in the greenhouse), Rose (her sister), Liz again (when she meets Jack)
- Chapter 3, Jack
- Chapter 4, Ian (the park manager)
- Zar, above, has his first third person appearance in Chapter 6.

You could have one third person character's viewpoint going through the whole book. That makes it quite like first person, the major difference is that the narrator (the author, you) can interrupt to put something right, say tell us something about family history, the area or whatever. Some books have a strong authorial voice. Charles Dickens is there in his third person novels, such as *A Christmas Carol*, and so is Roald Dahl with his wry voice, taking the mickey out of adults.

A fairy tale with one third person character's viewpoint is Jack and the Beanstalk. He is present all the time, from swapping the cow for the beans, to climbing the beanstalk, to stealing the giant's hen, until the final scene with him chopping down the tree. Many fairy tales are told this way.

Mostly though, in novels with the third person viewpoint, you have a number of viewpoint characters. For a writer, this helps to develop the character as you are seeing the world through their eyes. But too many switches in point of view, from character A to B to C to D, especially early on, can be annoying for the reader. You must get the story going, pile on the conflict, so the reader wants to read on.

Irritated with too many changes of viewpoint, a reader may well close the book permanently.

You may have noticed that in the example, in chapter 2 I began with Liz (in her house, having breakfast, thinking about her painting and her age). Then I switched (with a double line break) to Rose, her sister, who Liz has kicked out, and is now sleeping secretly in the bowling green pavilion. Another double line break and back to Liz when we have the beginnings of a romance between her and Jack.

You can switch point of view within a chapter, though it took me some time to get the confidence to do this.

The Way It Works

With third person, say with Jack, the reader only sees what he sees and hears, only gets his thoughts. In the first chapter, Jack's encounter with the manager at the park gate, we know what Jack is thinking, but not the manager's thoughts, although we know a fair bit through his words and body language. This is true to life. If I am talking to you, I can only be certain about my own thoughts and hope that you are being truthful.

I could have given *my* thoughts as narrator, say about the history of the park. But I want to get the story moving, and set up the conflict between the manager and Jack from the beginning. This is not the place for extra information.

A Problem

In crime novels, there is a specific difficulty with third person narration. You have to be honest with your reader, so suppose Fred has killed Alice and he is being interviewed by the police. But he's just one of a number of your suspects. If we wrote the police interview third person from Fred's point of view, then we would have him denying the killing, lying to them about his whereabouts and so forth. But his thoughts would reveal him as the killer. He'd be chewing over such thoughts as 'I hope they don't find the knife', 'John had better back up my alibi', 'I hope I cleaned all the blood out of the car'.

If the writer doesn't want the reader to know that Fred is the killer, they should write that scene third person from the police interviewer's point of view. Then Fred's thoughts are not revealed to readers.

Here's a trick of the trade. A way to guess who did the murder in a novel is to concentrate on the main characters not allowed a third person chapter after the murder. The writer doesn't want them revealing their thoughts. (I could be drummed out of the Crime Writers Association for that revelation).

Omniscient Narrator

This is one I did, without knowing I was doing it, in that mess of a first book. The one I abandoned. It's hard, too easy to do it badly. I was jumping from character to character, giving their thoughts and views, but quite inconsistently, not knowing what I was doing.

The omniscient narrator has complete freedom, which is not all it is cracked up to be. You could reveal all the thoughts of every character in every chapter. Boy, would your book be long and languid. Unless you are a great writer. If not, you must be choosy and that's the difficulty with this mode. Choose who, and when.

Dickens does it sometimes. He is a great writer but even he can ramble away, losing tension, as he goes from character to character. I don't know a crime writer who uses this point of view, so my advice is don't use it. Stick with first person or third person.

Necessity

You have to decide whether it's first person or third (forget omniscient narrator) before you can settle on a single line. With *Hard Cash*, I used first person all the way through. I had no doubts. In the *Jack of All Trades* crime series, I use third person, following Jack about half the time, and other characters the rest.

You could try the first paragraph or two in first person, and then try them again in third person. See which you prefer. But you are going to have to make a decision to get much further.

Once the decision is made and you are writing, imagine your reader as you write. Be aware, be clear. You have to satisfy more than yourself as you are writing to be appreciated by readers, alone with your book.

EXERCISE 10

Write a piece in the first person. Say 500 words. Now change this to third person, add a few authorial thoughts.

CHAPTER 12: Thought

Characters judge, assess, smile at you when they are planning to kill you, drinking a coffee contemplating suicide, deciding whether to tell you about their lottery win. We think all the time in our waking hours. And asleep, if troubled we dream, which is thinking of a sort.

We may be put upon by our boss, and say yes sir, no sir, but that doesn't stop us thinking sir is a tyrant. Or we may be so cowed that we censor our thoughts, like living under a dictatorship where a word out of place can lead to arrest. So we cull forbidden thought. But thought is unavoidable, even if it's just thoughts of how afraid we are.

As much as speech, perhaps more so, thought gives us a character. The real person behind the mask. The murderer may lie their head off, but their thoughts, if only we could read those thoughts, a lot of time, and lives, would be saved. If we were telepathic, we'd know at once who the killer was, without all the expense of forensics, and the everlasting questioning of the suspects.

But you, the author, have a superpower. You can read thoughts. (I shall avoid you at a party, not that I've killed anyone. But you know that already.)

Here are Rose's thoughts. She's Liz's sister, if you recall. Rose is not having a good time, sleeping secretly in the bowling pavilion, and working on the leafvac too, a machine she hates.

She was vaccing the edge, where the lawn met the shrubbery. Rose stopped and felt the leaf bag. Five minutes maybe and it'd be full. She'd like to empty it now, get a break from the noise and death images, take her time at the dump, but Ian had seen her at the leaf mould pound, emptying a less than full bag last time, and given her a tongue lash. Five minutes of belch and roar to endure.

She'd tried out music and headphones on Friday. Useless in this racket. She'd have to get those really expensive noise cancelling ones. Except it seemed like a sort of cowardice, a denial. Like spraying a manure heap with lavender. It was still there under the smell.

This would be her hell, the one in waiting for her. Like what's-his-name with the big rock. She'd be given this massive vac, to suck in evildoers until the end of time. She'd empty the bag into a vast cauldron of boiling pitch, go back and find the path as full of sinners as it was before.

The machine was sucking just under a holly tree when she saw it. The leaves shot into the machine, clearing a space, and there it was - a hand. She leaped back. Help! It was in her head, dead bodies - and there was one, or rather a bit of one, a hand and wrist. Rose turned off the machine. And bent down warily for a closer look. The hand was in a sleeve. So not just a cut off hand, a gangland job. It was attached to a body. What should she do?

She folded the hand back at the elbow so she couldn't see it. Dead bodies are dead. She could just carry on, pretend she hadn't seen it. And let some old woman with a dog snuffle it out. She turned on the vac and began sucking her way on, away from the holly and its secret.

And then stopped.

If she reported a dead body, she'd get a break. A good break, and a pat on the back. No one could tell her off for being a concerned, solid citizen and reporting an actual corpse in the park. And she'd have an exciting tale for a week. Guess what I found in the park? she'd tell her clubbers in the chill-out room. She'd leave out the leaf vaccing bit, but maybe not, they might find it suitably apoca-lyptic. Or she could make it sound like a blast. Being all on your own, with your thoughts, minding your own business, when a hand comes out of the leaves… Honest.

Better check first though. She turned off the vac and went back to the holly bush. Rose got down on her knees and looked under the canopy. And saw a grimy face looking back at her.

Not a word is spoken here. We have Rose's thoughts as she pushes her leafvac through the autumn leaves. She resents the manager, Ian, for putting her on this job. And is yearning for her tea break. In our heads each of us is meaner, more selfish, we don't have to put on an act to show how good and reasonable we are. The words in our heads would shock our mothers. Thank heavens they are locked in, and our voices know how to censor.

Sexual thoughts, criminal thoughts, swear words, what a gamut of the forbidden parade our minds. We are not as nice as we like to be seen to be.

Here's Jack, working away, bricklaying:

He glanced at his watch. Twenty minutes
to tea break. Over in the greenhouse with
Liz. Steamy biscuits. Oh yes. He tried
not to think of what might happen after
the last biscuit melted in the tea.
Nothing most likely. She might be fixed
up, a big bruising guy, a 10th Dan in
some martial arts discipline involving
flying kicks and punches that smashed
planks in half. Or. There was the dream,
the one he was a sucker for. His bedmate,
the companion of his soul, the one and
only… And he wondered if he was too
awkward a bugger for that to ever really
happen. Once he'd got off best behaviour,
once he was seen for what he really was.
A builder scraping a living, a drink away
from a drunken sot; she'd run a mile.
  Women aren't perfect. That had to be
remembered. We are all dirty sinners,
dressing up, washing and deodorising to
give the lie to the lonely ape howling
for love. Some of the guys at Alcohol
Halt had it all down as original sin. The
wicked trip of all humanity, with only
one way to salvation.
  The problem with dating, and such like,
was that everyone was on best behaviour,
making you think: I'm the only one
pretending. Junk, pure junk, he knew. But
he found at times it was hard to convince
himself.

Here's sexual thoughts, fantasy. Some writers would be a lot cruder than I am, balancing the realistic and the exaggerated to hold the reader by their fantasies. Though some readers' thoughts are porn, fed by porn. I'm not writing for such people, nor are most crime writers. Some violence, some sex, but not so much of the latter that it takes over the story. Kills it in fact.

Pornography has poor plots. I go for romance to leaven the dirty deeds.

Jack is trying not to think of what might happen when he visits Liz in her greenhouse, but we are not in total control of our thoughts. Tolstoy tells a tale of himself as a small boy, being told to go into the corner and not think of the white bear. The poor boy can't do it of course.

There are ways, though, to control our thoughts. I find a chess game works, it so totally involves me, I can't think of anything else. A sport too can be that involving. Though we could be on a treadmill in a gym, running hard, and still with dreams of winning the London Marathon. So we have headphones too, playing loud rock music to drown out the voice in our head.

But if you have just committed a murder, there's a voice that's hard to quell, unless you are a psychopath – then guilt does not undo you, and you can tidy up coherently. Still, fear of getting caught can obsess even this malefactor.

Thought enriches your storytelling, deepens your characterisation. It is especially important for main characters. Have too little and they come over as paper thin. Get them thinking, all the time, like we do, and your characters and storytelling will be all the richer.

CHAPTER 13: How to Begin

I t's not easy to answer how and when to begin writing, as writers have different modes. The detailed planners will only start once they have planned the book from A to Z. They'll know the characters and what is going to happen in every chapter. Such complete planning is unusual, I am sure. Raymond Chandler said: *If you gave me the best plot in the world all worked out I could not write it. It would be dead for me.*

That's me too, and a surprising number of other writers, sometimes referred to as seat of the pants writers, which is another way of saying you get writing without knowing where you are going. It is surprisingly common. Ultra-planning is uncommon. What it means for me, is that once I've done a fair bit of thinking about the setting and the work Jack is doing, some scratchings on possible characters, I'll begin. I don't know the plot, though I do know someone will be murdered along the way.

I start, invariably, with my main character, Jack, and begin to lay trails. To where, I don't know. A path begins opening up, which goes somewhere and might be worth following. A book works on the readers' curiosity. It has to keep readers wanting to know what will happen or they'll put the book down and watch TV.

Events, thoughts. I need some romance, some conflict. His daughter is sure to be in trouble at school...

Once curiosity begins to pall, then brilliant writing can still keep a reader on the page, superb characterisation may be enough too. But this is great writer land, not where most of us live. We need tension between the characters and a strong plot. The reader needs to feel the book is going somewhere.

The beginning, though, concerns us here. The first page or so. How to grip the reader.

Here's the beginning of *Jack at Death's Door:*

Jack drove slowly through the wrought-iron gates. The thick pillars on either side had church steeple tops. He stopped ten yards further on, outside the cemetery office, a stout, grey stone, single storey building. A serious edifice to deal with the serious business of disposing of the dead. Jack didn't feel altogether comfortable working in a cemetery, having absorbed the superstitions associated with coffins, bones and graveyards. He only ever came here for funerals. The grounds had a solemnity, a sadness, mingled with the awareness of his own mortality and fear of what was underground. But it was daytime, and ghosts strolled after dark. Work was work. And he needed it. The van needed repairing, the maintenance he was paying Alison for his daughter, Mia, would drain his account this month. There was the mortgage coming up. He'd work in hell if he was paid in advance.

Jack leaned back in his van and rubbed his eyes. He hadn't slept well, but employment had got him out of bed. His obligation was to do X so he could get paid Y, in order to pass it on to A, B

and C. Grubby lucre, going in and out of
the bank, who assured him in their ads he
was their only purpose on earth. But
wouldn't give him a loan. Probably just
as well, as he'd have to pay it back and
have even less money in the months to
come.

Ring a ring of roses, pass the greasy
notes.

He was in a grim mood. The trick was to
get working, to forget the nexus of
obligations. Engage with saw and hammer,
create order from timber, brick and
nails. The beginning was the leap, to
make purpose out of a meagre fuel of a
slice of toast and a cup of tea. He must
make the first steps. Talk to the man.
Look like a builder in control of tools
and materials who knew exactly where to
cut the wood and how to lay concrete.

Maria had pulled the rug from under him
yesterday evening. He'd just showered to
go out to dinner with her, when her text
came.

'It's not working, Jack. I was going to
tell you over dinner, but why waste money
on good food? Sorry to do it this way,
but I don't like scenes.'

Maria doesn't like scenes, but she has made one for Jack, in
the cemetery, a little nervous about working among grave-
stones. Although he is a character that has gone through a
number of novels, I have to assume that there will be
readers where this is the first Jack novel they have come
across. And there will be others who haven't read about Jack
for say a couple of years and so need a reminder of who he
is. So I tell you here, or remind you, in my beginning, that

Jack is a builder, broke and with debts. But he has work to do, even if his girlfriend has spurned him. There's pain, but the world must still be faced.

A builder is not just a builder. There's the rest of his existence, the totality that makes a human being. A life beyond work, with relationships, dreams, disappointments and the ever present necessity to pay bills.

Enough of that. I must create conflict. There's some with the girlfriend (ex) and I do decide to bring her back, just to confuse Jack. To complicate his life. Don't ever make it easy for your main character, rather pile it on. You'll get much more out of it. So, a rotten start to the day for Jack. It gets worse when he goes into the office to tell the manager he is on site, and meets hostility. The man does not want him there. Pretty soon, Jack realises that the cemetery is run by a family fighting amongst themselves for control.

That didn't come to me at once, the family conflict. But I felt a weakness in the story, and stopped to think how I could toughen it. And remembered the mantra: family, family, family.

We all have families. For some, occasions like Christmas are hell. We know of sibling rivalry, hatred of a mother or father, friction between parents, interfering uncles, aunts and grandparents. It has been the stuff of fiction from the Greek dramatists to the ongoing present.

In this tale, someone will be killed. At this point, I don't know who will, or who does the killing. I didn't know for quite some time. But once I had decided on family owner-ship, I had my grip on the novel.

Pile on the conflict. I can't say that too often. And keep moving forward. Jack is about to meet the young woman on the flower stall. Some romance, a rest from conflict. But heavens, she's one of the family too!

Don't Keep Reading It!

That was one of the best writing tips I ever got. If every day before you start writing, you go back to the beginning and read through the lot, that is going to take you longer and longer as you get further in. It will be an increasing waste of writing time. On top of this, in quite a short time, you'll be sick of the book as you have read the same pages over and over.

This is what I do. To start my writing day, I go back a few pages and edit them. No more than a few pages. That editing gets me into writing gear, and on I go. The big advantage of doing this is that when you finish the first draft, a lot of the book, say the first 2/3rds, will be fresh when you come to read it for rewrites, enabling you to be more objective.

Summary

You have your notes on your main character and the setting. About some of the other characters too, even if somewhat sketchily. If not sure about what point of view to write in, go for third person; most crime writers do.

Your main character has something to do that day. Decide exactly what, and get them moving. What's the weather like? Heap on the conflict as they interact with other characters. Think family, family, family, like an ancient Greek dramatist. Their own and the family of others. Have a row with someone.

We are all looking for love. The married stray too, you know. And someone, along the way, will get murdered.

CHAPTER 14: A
Chapter on Time

I t took you some time to get here. Chapter 14. The seconds are ticking by as you read on. And that novel you will be writing takes place over a period of time. Banal thoughts perhaps, so banal we barely think about it. Or the time as you write, conflicting with all the other things you have to get done. Appointments, dates, dry cleaner, DIY. Time is not elastic. We have alarm clocks, tea breaks, lunch hours, anniversaries, birthdays, the sun rises and sets and there's more yet to do. We swim in time like fish in water. It is ever there, ticking on.

It stalks the crime novel. '*Where were you between 9 and 11 o'clock last night?*' says the detective to the prime suspect. They had better have their lies prepared with witnesses ready to vouch they were with him playing cards between those hours.

The forensic pathologist when taking the rectal temperature of the body is attempting to get as close as possible to the time of death. Hours in court are spent talking about time, where the accused was, what they were doing, who else was there. What time they left and what time they came back.

Seconds, minutes, hours, days and weeks.

Time Scale

What period of time does your novel cover? Crime novels usually have a shortish time scale. Time is money, goes the cliché. That doesn't stop it being true, especially for the police force. If there's no result in a month or two they will cut down, or disband, the Major Incident Team. The private eye will cease being paid if she can't get a result in a reasonable time. Depending on the pocket of their client.

There's reader time too. I get impatient if the novel is too slow. What does 'slow' mean? Too much of my time passing and nothing much happening. I want to be gripped so I don't think about the time I am wasting on this wretched book. I have alternatives, you know, like close the book and watch TV.

The author in panic can take Raymond Chandler's advice:

'When in doubt, have a man come through the door with a gun in his hand.'

That gives you more time. Spend it wisely.

Dealing with days and weeks

If nothing much is happening, writer, don't stick around. Move on to when something is happening.

You can dispose of time quickly by writing such things as, 'By the next week, he had...' Or move on a month, if needs be, in a paragraph. A new chapter can push time on. Readers are familiar with such time changes.

With my young adult novel, *Half a Bike*, I felt my draft was slow, lacking bite. So I ripped out four middle chapters. A tough thing to do as there was some good writing there, but I felt something drastic had to be done. In poetry they call it 'drowning your babies'. A ruthless metaphor suitable for crime writing too. In drama scripts, one is urged 'not to be precious', meaning don't hang onto a part that drags just because there's some good writing. Cut to the chase.

In the case of *Half a Bike*, I had jettisoned a whole day. It certainly tightened up the manuscript. I searched through the manuscript to catch any inconsistencies, and I thought I'd got them all. But the editor at Faber was puzzled by one I'd missed, as it was referring to the wrong day. I told her about the deleted chapters and then made the correction I'd missed.

Time of Year

The seasons affect the setting. Hot in summer perhaps, or an unseasonal chill, cold and windy in winter, with snow and sleet. Leaves turning and blowing in autumn. There might be daffodils in early spring. Consider bird song, flowers, the sound of the lawn mower, the state of the sky with fleeting clouds, or glaring blue. In the bleak midwinter, it's cold and frosty, the skeletal trees point out the corpses of dead birds.

Or there's a midsummer drought, with the lawn burnt brown, a burial revealed perhaps. Or a forest fire, and the detective and murderer caught up in it.

Period

When is your novel set? Is it now? Or the 60s, pre-war, Edwardian, Victorian? History is your oyster, providing you know your stuff.

We live in the present and write in the present. But what was the present ceases to be the present with every tick of the clock. I wrote about Jack going to a nearby coffee shop full of paintings and social workers. Or so he imagines them to be. The coffee shop was a real place. Well, the book is out there, but the coffee bar has closed. History is relentless, like the waves eating up the beach, it doesn't stop.

Age

Peter Pan never grows old. Neither does James Bond. But sadly actors do, so Bond has done his share of shape-shifting in his movies, beginning in the 1960s to well into the 21st century (whenever you read this). If Bond had aged, he would be in his 90s at the time of writing. But it is imperative he stays young, in his 40s at the max, to be the handsome sex symbol, muscular and quick on his feet, that the films require. So change the actors, discard the last one like a mouldy orange. But what about modernity? A possibility was to keep Bond in a period, say the 60s, but the movies delight in ultra modern technologies which denies that option. So the movie moguls have granted him the elixir of youth as time sweeps on.

I don't know any crime novel series that have gone that way, keeping the main character the same age over many decades. Ruth Rendell, though, had to take years off Inspector Wexford. He first appears, in his 40s, in the 1964 novel *From Doon with Death*. His last case was *No Man's Nightingale* in 2013, which is more than 50 years later, well beyond police retirement age. Rendell quietly reduced his age, though he is semi-retired in the last books. I've not seen any complaints, so it seems such liberties are allowable.

Ian Rankin plays it straight with his detective Inspector Rebus. He's been ageing from the first book, published in 1987. Currently he's in his 60s and coming to the end of his time in the force. Though consultancy is an option. Or freeze time for a while. Authors have such powers.

I have not given the exact age of my main character, Jack. His daughter though has aged from 10 to 14 in the series, so he must be four years older too. Mid to late 30s, I grant. I will have to decide how quickly to age him. Whether to stand still a while or let the years roll on.

So, thoughts for you. How old is your main character? How old might they be at the end of your series, when you are old and famous?

Time and the Series

It takes time to write a series, and keeping it going can be a strain. Arthur Conan Doyle grew weary of his Sherlock Holmes tales. Although he was writing other books, all the public wanted was Holmes. So in 1893, Conan Doyle killed him off. He had Holmes and his arch enemy, Moriarty, fight above the Reichenbach Falls. There was a narrow path to the ledge where they were seen wrestling. Both had gone when Watson got there. Two sets of footprints going out and none returning.

Holmes was dead!

The public were distraught. But Conan Doyle could get on with writing his historical fiction. The fight at the Reichenbach Falls is related in T*he Final Problem*, the last story in *The Memoir of Sherlock Holmes*, free on Project Gutenberg.

There was a clamour for more tales. But for ten years, Conan Doyle pushed them aside. Until in 1903, he relented and Holmes was brought back to life in *The Adventure of the Empty House*. Conan Doyle had had a much needed break from his detective. Energised, he could set him off on new cases.

How Holmes was brought back to life is a spoiler. Worth a read as it's a classic tale, the first in *The Return of Sherlock Holmes*, available free on Project Gutenberg and similar sites for out of copyright works.

The ten year break enabled Conan Doyle to get his mojo back. And to accept that Sherlock Holmes was going to be his major creation, in terms of reputation and income. The full canon of the Sherlock Holmes stories consist of four novels and 56 short stories, the last one written in 1927, forty years after the first. More than half of the short stories were written after the break.

Writers often take time off from a series. Perhaps like Patricia Cornwell writing some true crime, in her case looking afresh at the Jack the Ripper murders in *Portrait of a Killer*. Getting away from your series can recharge the batteries. Or it may mean the series has come to an end, and it's time for the author to find a new writing project.

Ruth Rendell often wrote one-offs between her Inspector Wexford novels. Ian Rankin had the difficulty that having decided to write the Inspector Rebus tales in real time, the Inspector was due for retirement. That couldn't be evaded and Rebus retired in 2007. In his break from Inspector Rebus, Rankin got involved in drama and began his Malcolm Fox series. Fox is in the Complaints Department of the Edinburgh police, investigating dodgy cops. Amongst whom is Rebus who doesn't always take the orthodox route. Having a second main character gave Rankin flexibility, and Rebus was brought back as a consultant.

Writing Time

Your time is finite. Day to day, you have enough on your plate. How long can you spend on writing? How long with a push? A full time job makes it hard, but many writers start that way, squeezing writing time in between work and family. Cyril Connolly has an often quoted warning:

'There is no more sombre enemy of good art than the pram in the hall.'

But an enemy can be beaten, and there are single parents who have done so. A prime example is JK Rowling in her early days. She was living on benefits with a child, and writing in cafes. We all know how that tale led to fortune.

That's not to say it isn't tough, and each child makes it tougher. But it's not for me to say whether you can do it or not. It's your battle.

How long does it take to write a novel?

That's the cliché question, asked of writers at festivals and school visits. (The other big one is: where do you get your ideas from?). My reply is that it depends. If the writing goes well, no snags, then about three months. If I have lots of problems then it could take me nine months.

But it's not a race. There are writers who take several years over each book. They don't have many books in their catalogue, but each one is quality. Alternatively, there are hacks who can churn one out in a month. Which would you rather be?

This is not necessarily a choice.

My first published book took me nine months to write because I was working full time. If I wasn't I could have done it in three months.

So what?

Don't get hung up; the only answer that matters is your own.

Write regularly

As opposed to sporadically. Find time each day to sit at your desk and write. Are you a night person or a morning person? I prefer mornings when I have a clear head and the problems of the day haven't kicked in. Some writers prefer late nights. Find your time, stick to it. Switch off your phone, tell your family you are writing for the next few hours. They may resent this, especially if you are having no success. Most writers start that way. You have to be selfish with your time. Or you won't get any writing done.

With my book *Hard Cash*, I was working as a community worker. I arose at 6 am and wrote for an hour every morning, before getting ready for work. I did some more after work. The book has to stay hot. Let it cool and you may lose all enthusiasm.

I don't read fiction when I'm writing. It takes up too much of my time. Besides which, I don't want someone else's characters in my head. I've only room for my own.

CHAPTER 15: Plot As You Go

lotting is an idiosyncratic activity. Experienced writers evolve their own ways. Some with lots of detail before they begin, others with scant detail. I have seen schemes in how-to books that left me scratching my head in puzzlement, though they evidently made sense to the writers as they weren't novices.

Well, this is my oddity which I call Plot As You Go. Which is not quite as simple as it sounds.

Authors rarely begin writing with nothing. I have given the example of *Murder at Any Price*, which wasn't quite 'nothing' but as close as you can get. If you recall, I had a man waking in a strange room, in bed with a dead, naked woman.

In writing that book, I began with an image, which I then had to make sense of. I needed to know who the man was and where he was. Did he know the woman? Gradually moving into coherence step by step.

Not too quickly, as its very mystery has a power. The reader is as befuddled as the writer, and really wants to know what on earth is going on.

So far so good.

The danger for the writer, in such circumstances, is that they can get stuck in a cul-de-sac with no way out. Or the story becomes tepid with explanation, losing that initial excitement. And the writer has nothing to fall back on, as no planning at all has been done.

But there are writers who use such methods for every book. That really is Plot As You Go *par excellence*. Starting with next to nothing, inventing characters on the hoof, realising the setting, making the chaotic sensible, and hopefully generating an engaging tale. Quite a feat.

I need more than that to get on the move. Fortunately, with a series, I have a fair bit before I write a single word. I have a builder, Jack Bell, who lives in a flat in Forest Gate, London. He has a van with Jack of All Trades on the side, a 14 year old daughter, Mia, who he parents with his ex-wife Alison. He has had a drink problem which he hopes he is free from, but there is the occasional relapse. His hobby is astronomy and he has a telescope.

Jack is single, heterosexual, in his mid-to-late 30s, and ever hopeful he will find a partner.

That is way above nothing. And there's more.

This is crime, so I know where he works there will be a murder. And some romance too. There will likely be a problem with his daughter, teenagers being teenagers. So already I have some idea of the main plot (the murder), and subplots (romance, and daughter problems). This is the power of a series. You don't start from scratch each time. You have your on-going characters, in a known setting.

You don't face the horror of the blank page.

He's a builder, so let's put him to work. In a place where there will be conflict (hence the murder) and a chance of romance. In *Jack on the Tower*, I chose two houses together. With just one house, I thought there would be insufficient suspects. The building work had to be believable. I decided he would be pointing brickwork on one of the houses. I researched pointing: the mortar used and tools. I decided he would use a scaffolding tower, one of those on wheels. Planking is shifted to different levels as he works on the wall, beginning at the top. When he has pointed that section, the

110

scaffolding tower is moved along. He goes to the top and continues pointing. He uses a block and tackle to bring up his mortar.

You may wonder why he starts pointing from the top and not from the bottom. Well, if he started from the bottom instead, then, as he rose higher, mortar would dribble down on brickwork he has already pointed. Starting from the top means he can clean off the dribbles as he comes down, and the brickwork above him stays clean.

I need to know such things. I might use it in the book, or I might not. Building work is his reality. I have to convince my reader. I need to know how to assemble a scaffolding tower, the materials and tools used for pointing (in this case), his worries about getting paid. But I can't just write about his work. I need to think who lives in the two houses. I haven't written a word of the novel as yet but my notes are growing.

I am getting impatient, though. Let's go.

And so, I begin writing. Jack arrives at the house and has to assemble the tower which has been delivered. Jack has trouble straight away with Feliks next door who insists Jack should pay him because the tower overlaps into his garden by a few feet. Feliks is working on the base of a shed at the back of his garden. The cement mixer rumbles away.

Great, conflict at once.

Feliks owns his house and has two tenants: a prostitute, Saffron, who he overcharges because he can. And an old lady, Sophie, in the basement. She hasn't been seen for some time and Trevor, her son, has come to find out why. I am making this up as I go along and it seems OK.

So that's Feliks' place, next door to where Jack is working. His clients' house is owned by a couple, Mike and Jean. Mike is an unemployed musician and dope head. Jean is a writer with growing success with her books and her online courses. They have a cleaner, Mandy, who Mike is screwing when his wife is away. Lots of conflict to get the tension ablaze.

I decided on a subplot with Alison, Jack's ex and the mother of Mia, their daughter. Unknown to Jack she has found Feliks on a computer dating site. And they have begun dating.

By around chapter 3, I have a cast and my setting. I know there is going to be romance with Jack. Most likely with the wife, Jean, as her marriage is on the ropes. Surely she will discover the cleaner and her husband in bed?

Well, I can guarantee that.

About this time, I interviewed some of the main characters: Mike, Jean, Mandy, Feliks and Saffron. This gave me a strong feeling for my cast. The interviews vary in length from 600 to 1000 words. Here's some snippets from the interviews.

- *So how do you see your life going, Jean?* [The wife]

'There's a question I reflect on too often. My marriage is finished. There's no saving it. But there's the house and there's Lily [the toddler] to consider. If we divorced, then we'd have to sell the house to divide the spoils. He might even get Lily, as he's been house-husband for the last 18 months. Courts are not predictable any more. I thought of splitting the house in two. Making two flats of it. But then I don't want to live on top of him, dealing with his garbage. No. I think I'll have to work hard for the next couple of years, build up my capital. And then divorce him. Except whatever I save, he could get half of. That lazy git. It's so unfair.'

- *Do you think you can carry on like this, in this house, Mike?* [Jean's husband]

'Why not? She's too busy to care. I look after her kid. Do the shopping. Mostly. Sort of. She'd complain whoever did it. It's about me, what I want to do. I've got to get my shit together. Might as well be here as anywhere else. And I've got Mandy and a spliff.'

- *How come you're a cleaner, Mandy?*

'It's because I can't get enough acting work. I work for an agency – and between acting work, I go out as a cleaner. You probably know I worked with Mike on *Liverpool Lullaby*. Jean doesn't know, or I wouldn't be here. Thinks I simply came through the agency. Sometimes I don't clean at all at their place, depends whether she's around. Or we do a quick scoot round in fifteen minutes together, post shag.'

- *How do you make a living, Feliks?* [the man next door]

'I'm a landlord. I have three houses. The one I live in, on Clova Road, one on Earlham Grove, one down in Plaistow. The Clova Road place houses me and two tenants. Saffron the whore. She pays well. The old lady, Sophie, who doesn't. Protected tenant. I hope she dies soon or maybe I'll help her along.'

- *Have you got a girlfriend, Feliks?*

'They come and go. I don't like them long term. You see, I like to enjoy life and they want to change you. If I want a screw, I go see Saffron. We do a deal on the rent. I use a dating website sometimes. I say I'm thinking of marriage, well you have to say that, but in this country, with its divorce laws, you'd have to be crazy. If I got married, then a few years later, she'd divorce me and take half my assets. Madness.'

Running Plot

Once I've got into the writing, and have some idea where I am going, I make a document called **After Chapter X** (where X is the chapter I have got to). I write in short summaries what has happened so far. Then I write a heading **Next**, and under that I write what I think will happen next. It may not be that far ahead.

Here it is, in simplified form. **So Far** would be quite a bit longer, but this is to illustrate the method rather than lose you in my shorthand.

After Chapter X

So Far

- Jack is up on the tower pointing

- Trevor has come to find his mother, and finds she is not in her flat

- Mike in bed with Mandy, caught by Jean while Jack babysits

- Mandy is fired

Next

- Mike with Mandy, tells her to come late morning tomorrow, he'll be out, so will Jean be out. Mandy can steal Jean's stuff, better take some of his for effect.

- Feliks with Saffron. Wants more rent. He hits her. She says she'll

call Benjy (her pimp) if he hits her
again

- Etc

Once I have written Chapter XI, I make a new document called **After Chapter XI**, and add what I've written that day in summary. I will move **Next** on, getting further ahead. Sometimes I have a lot of 'Next' and sometimes not much.

After Chapter XI

- Jack is up on the tower pointing

- Trevor has come to find his mother, and finds she is not in her flat

- Mike in bed with Mandy, caught by Jean while Jack babysits

- Mandy is fired

- Mike with Mandy, tells her to come late morning tomorrow, he'll be out, so will Jean be out. Mandy can steal Jean's stuff, better take some of his for effect.

Next

- Feliks with Saffron. Wants more rent. He hits her. She says she'll call Benjy (her pimp) if he hits her again

- Mike and Jean big row, as Jean is going out to see Jack.

- Mia arriving at Jack's, talk with Jack about school, about computer dating etc, begins reading Jean's book.

- Etc

The actual writing of the novel for the day stops at **Next**. After **Next** I am working out how the story continues. If a chapter is long, I might save a document called, say, **Mid Chapter XII**.

Note, I can't see to the end yet. I think of writing the novel like walking in a fog up a mountain. Shapes come out of the mist as I walk on, clearing and becoming crags, huts, sheep or people. They disappear behind me, and new crags and people gradually come into view. Until we get to the summit.

If the summit is the murder, well, that brings in the cops and the investigation. I have so much at that point, I'll have no trouble plotting as I go.

This is one way of working. Try it if you wish, or adapt it for your own needs. I know these things are idiosyncratic. This method is only any good to you if it works. I hope it is clearer than some of the others I have come across.

CHAPTER 16: How to Write a Page Turner

A page turner is a book you don't want to put down. A book you'll stay up till the early hours to finish. It is compelling. It has got its hooks into you.

How does a novel do this?

Human beings are primitive. Like kittens, we are endlessly curious. And that is what a writer has to key into. Keep the reader curious.

We do this by various means. By having unanswered questions; a character might have a secret past, you can drop hints but you are in no hurry to say what it is. Make the reader wait. Think of the toys, wrapped up under the Christmas tree, how a child wants to know what is in hers. She keeps looking, Mum gives the odd clue, but the child has to wait till Xmas morning.

You might allow her to open one present, just one. But what's in the others? It's primitive, but get the hang of it. Create tension and hold it.

Make 'em wait. Let that be the motto above your desk.

Let's take Chandler's advice, as the story is slowing, and bring in the man with a gun. He could instantly shoot X dead, an important character. I'd give you one out of ten for that. Curiosity never had a chance to get going. So, let's have X running and hiding, the gunman searching, saying his nasty spiel, give us X's thoughts as he darts from place to place. The gunman shoots from time to time, to remind us he can.

You may still decide to kill X off, or you may be making time for other things to happen. The gunman might wound X but panic at some noise, the police perhaps. Your story has room for variations. An emotion has to be held to be effective.

Tension is the backbone of the crime novel. Don't instantly kill it.

In the police procedural, if tension is flagging, a common ruse is another murder. The equivalent of the man with the gun. You could make it the murder of the prime suspect. Then you have everyone flummoxed, but I hope not the writer. That's another element of the page turner: surprise. In this case a killing of someone the reader picked out as the killer.

The surprise could be someone who turns up who is supposed to be dead. Or a suspect who turns out to be an undercover cop, or a man and woman who are secretly brother and sister...

Threats

A threat works wonders in the tension department. A letter is a good way to deliver it. Better than an email. Though that can be stark enough. But if someone sends you a letter, then they know your address. Let us suppose it is a crude message, made up of individual letters cut out of a newspaper saying: *Beware the Ides of March!* Somewhat tame, you might feel, without sight of the conspirators.

So how about a concrete threat. This letter falls onto the mat one morning, with the following message:

```
Your wife gets it, unless you hand over
              the key. Love Hyde.
```

Where on earth do you start with that? What is the key? (I have no idea). Is it just a crank? Do you go to the cops? Do you tell your family? I'd do all of them to complicate things. To have other people reacting. A family row. And I'd get searching for the key.

Here's a piece from *Jack by the Hedge* with a threat. It's a number of chapters in, so I need to put you in the picture: Ian, the manager of the park, is talking to Liz, the greenhouse worker. She and he had a short relationship that she broke off. Ian speaks first. He has been delving in the files.

```
'You lied on your application form.'
   'OK, suppose I did. Spell it out. What
does it mean?'
   'When HR find out, they'll fire you. No
excuses will work. A lie is a lie. You'll
be out on your ear.'
   'Cashiered and disgraced,' she said
with a long sigh. 'I'll have to move out
of my cottage.' It had suddenly hit her.
'I'll get a lousy reference - and be
lucky to get a job stacking shelves in a
supermarket.' She appealed to her
manager. 'If you expose me, Ian, I'll
never get another job in this field… It
would be my career over. You know how I
love my cottage. You know I'm good at my
job. Be reasonable, Ian.'
   'Be reasonable to me then.'
   She was quiet for a few seconds, before
looking him in the eye. 'What do you
want?'
   'I want us to be engaged, Liz.'
   She sank back in the chair and breathed
out heavily. 'Right. I think I've got the
picture. Though it's all a bit much for
me right now. I'm overwhelmed. It's all
somewhat sudden, hitting me all at once.
```

Hell. It was going so well. Too well.'
She scratched the side of her face. 'I
need to go away and think about it, Ian.'
   'I'll give you the morning.'
   'And then what?' She flapped her hands
rapidly. 'Don't tell me. I've heard too
much already.' She took a deep breath.
'Right. Lunchtime. I know where it's at.
More or less.' She stood up and strode
rapidly to the door. 'I'll give you an
answer at one o'clock. Promise me you
won't do anything before.'
   'I won't.'
   'Thank you for small mercies.'
And she left him.

Ian is blackmailing her. She must agree to marry him or
he'll expose her lying to get the job. And that will mean
she'll get fired, losing her job, her park house and getting a
bad reference too. But a blackmail threat can rebound. It's a
threat to the blackmailer too. Liz has few choices: she can
get engaged to Ian, or she can call his bluff and risk the sack
and losing her house. But this is a crime novel, do you recall
those mushrooms? You've probably forgotten them.

Liz hasn't.

Liz says she'll give her answer at lunchtime. That's over
three hours' time. She is making him wait, and I am making
the reader wait. During that time, there will be other hares
set running. Something is going on in the children's playground where money is passing hands, the Mayor is coming
to plant a tree, Liz has invited Jack to the greenhouse for his
tea break...

The main plot and sub plots interweave. The main plot
is the one with Liz and the manager, the sub plots are a
burgeoning romance between Jack and Liz, an illegal Ponzi

scheme going on in the children's playground, and Zar will leave home because his family find out he is gay.

This novel is not a whodunit. It is clear to the reader who did the killing, but will they get away with it?

With a whodunit there must be sufficient suspects to keep the reader guessing. All with good motives. That's the page turning aspect. *Jack at Death's Door,* which is set in a cemetery, has a murder with multiple suspects. They are the family, who are the owners of the cemetery, plus a few externals to complicate matters. The need to know is one element holding the reader. Though it shouldn't be the only thing left. Too many times, I have lost interest in the characters; I simply want to know who did it. So I skip 100 pages and read the last chapter to find out. The book, though, has failed.

In summary

A page turner has interweaving plots with threats, romance perhaps, questions unanswered for a while, sufficient suspects (in a whodunit). Surprise is a card you can play at any time: killing the prime suspect, a surprise witness or relationship, DNA ruling someone out, an unexpected fingerprint...

All these have to work with characters the reader is interested in. They hold us, beyond the puzzles and surprises. Some we will despise, others we care about and hope they come through.

Endings

I'm not about to give away my endings. To do that is to break a prime rule in the writer's lexicon. It's the spoiler of spoilers. Instead I will give you some stats from the novels in my series.

Three killers get away with it. The reader knows they did it. You must be fair on your reader. Or they'll complain, and hit you with one star on Amazon. In two of these novels, the killers had reasons for their crime which the reader can sympathise with. A novel does not have to comply with the law of the land but with the law of novel writing. Like fairy stories, where when the baddy is murdered, no one grieves. The moralist is troubled with this. But this is fiction, I'm not encouraging murder.

In the third novel, the murder is a clever one, Jack knows who did it, we know too but there isn't the evidence for the police. So the perpetrator gets away with it. This is not unlike real life. Some murderers don't get caught. And some innocent people do time, and even get executed where they have the death penalty.

In another three of the novels, the killers die at the end. This has always been a popular way of finishing a crime novel, especially if there is insufficient evidence. Then justice is served, sort of. Cowboy justice. A killer is in a coma at the end of another, and the reader will be quite content if he stays that way.

Three cases go to trial. With strong evidence against the defendants.

That's the muster of my novels, the murders all sorted out, one way or another. Sub plots have to be tied up too. For Jack this could be his romance, though sometimes the woman is murdered or she is the killer. Either way, this ends his romantic interlude. In a couple, she isn't dead or a killer, so the love interest can continue. An upbeat last chapter. But it stops between books. At the beginning of the next, he is unattached.

Other characters have their storylines which should have some sort of ending. As the novel proceeds, you need to be thinking about the story arc of each important character. Not the minor characters, but those who spend some time with us. You can't just abandon them. The reader wants to know what happens to them. There's not just one story in a good novel.

A satisfying ending leaves the reader with a feeling of completion, albeit a slight sorrow that the book is over. We have lived with the novel for half a dozen enjoyable hours, followed the various characters through their ups and downs. And now it's over.

Not quite.

They might give you a good review. And just as importantly, look forward to your next book.

CHAPTER 17: After the First Draft

You've finished the first draft. Take a break. Have a cup of tea. You deserve it. You've reached the endpoint. Or let's say the first endpoint. I'll grant you some time off.

How many words is your draft? There are publishers who say they won't accept a book shorter than 55k words. I find this harsh, somewhat arbitrary, and don't see the sense in it. A good novel of 40k can be very satisfying as opposed to a poor one at 80k, which might be all the better for extensive cuts. But it's their bat, their ball and if you want to play with them you have to accept their rules.

Word count is of less concern to authors who self-publish. It will affect the price. But this is not a book on marketing. And you haven't finished writing.

Having written the first draft, you have a choice on what to do next. Either give it a read through yourself, after a week or so off, while making notes. Then make your corrections. Or you may have a beta reader who will give it a read through and give their opinion. The other option is leave the draft for a while longer.

I go for the latter and leave my first draft for about five weeks. The reason I do this is that, having left the draft for a period, I can read it with some freshness. If I attempted to read it straight after finishing the writing, I would be too soaked in it to be able to judge it objectively.

During my five weeks off, I read books. Mostly crime, but I can stray into other areas and non-fiction too. I'm taking a holiday, after my three months of writing. I'm charging up my creative batteries.

At the end of the period, I go back to the first draft and I read it slowly. Our aim as writers is to be objective about our own work, as objective as we might be about another's. That's never quite possible as it is our own work, and we are prejudiced. We want it to be good, which is a danger. Nevertheless, I have found that by leaving the piece for five weeks at least, I can be fairly objective. I certainly know if it's bad. That hits me quickly.

Other things become apparent. Like how long it takes to draw me in. The draft could be too slow to get on the move. That means I'm going to have to do some cutting in, say, the first four chapters.

The story might hold me straight away. It is a good feeling to read a chapter and think, that was pleasing. However did I manage it? There is the reverse, when I think: that chapter doesn't work at all. And the best thing then is not to tinker with it, but throw it away and rewrite it. That takes some gumption, but otherwise you won't get away from the first version.

After the Reread

If you mostly like it, great. Go in and improve it. Adding paragraphs, perhaps description, judicious cutting, clarifying, and improving the style.

If you are unsure about the draft, that's certainly a big clue that things are not right. How far not right? Is it irredeemable? This is where a beta reader can come in very useful. A beta reader is your first choice to read your draft. Called beta because you are the alpha reader. They should not be your partner or spouse. I've made this mistake. I got my partner to read it, and when she didn't like it, I was hurt. It affected our relationship for a while. I never did that again. You need someone who is not so close to you. It could be a mutual thing with another writer. She is the beta reader for yours, you for hers.

Beta Readers

As they are your first readers, you want them to tell you what is right and wrong with your draft. That's a tall order. Editors get well paid for doing exactly that. Which means you have to be choosy with your beta readers.

You want your beta reader to read crime. It's no good if they only read romance. Their reading doesn't have to be nothing but crime, but they should read a fair amount of it. That's the league you want to join.

You want someone whose judgement is sound. That is so important. You don't want them misdirecting you, telling you to rewrite something which is fine. At this point you are vulnerable and it's too easy to take bad advice. So you have to be tough minded in your choice of beta readers. A poor beta reader is worse than no beta reader.

What do you do if you don't know anyone suitable?

There are online writers' groups, there may be a writers' group in your area, there are professional editors. Good editors are costly. Frequently, a first novel just doesn't work. So I suggest you try for beta readers by hook or by crook. At least you'll save money if your book is a dud.

Poor compensation, I know.

Writers' Groups

Before you take the route to professional services, try a writers' group. For many years, I was a member of Newham Writers Workshop. We met in a church crypt. And I could read up to 3000 words of my novel at a session. But only when it was my turn which was about one week in four. You get to know the other writers well, and informally you could ask one whose judgement you trust to be your beta reader.

If there's no local writers' group you can attend, then try online. Here's some I found on a brief perusal:

- Kboards Writers Cafe
- Absolute Write Water Cooler
- Reddit Writing Groups
- Insecure Writers Support Group
- Alliance of Independent Authors

There are many others. You simply need to Google 'Writers Group' and quite a few will come up. I suggest joining before you finish your novel, and getting involved by helping other writers. That's how these groups work: you help me and I'll help you. Mutual aid. You might find a useful ongoing partnership. She's your first reader, you are hers.

It is preferable to ask someone in the group directly if they will beta read your draft, someone you know has good judgement. You may strike lucky, or they may be too busy. But don't ask, don't get. Failing that, you'll have to put out a call to the group for a beta reader. That's risky as you could get some bad critics. With luck you'll get a few who offer to read your draft, and between their critiques you are able to get the feel of what your book needs.

What you want from your beta reader(s) is for them to read the draft and give an honest assessment. That's hard to do (and hard to take) but you want to enter the professional world, so you have to be judged in those terms. Of course, you may have a good book, let's hope so, with just minor changes necessary.

Before Sending It Out

Do the basics. Like spellcheck. It's surprising how many people don't. Following that, you must do your best to get your punctuation correct. There are online punctuation sites. I prefer a book and use the *Penguin Guide to Punctuation*. Common mistakes are: putting speech marks in the wrong place, misusing apostrophes, and not understanding semicolons. You can read up on these in an hour or so. You want your draft to be an easy read. Why irritate your beta reader with your continual use of the grocer's apostrophe?

Have a double space between paragraphs, and a page break between chapters. If you are sending your draft to your beta reader as a Word document, have the font at least 12 point. Your page should look clean, so there are no obstacles in the reader's way.

Editorial Services

You only want to go this way, if you believe there is a good book there that just needs help in its genesis. Before sending your work out to professional services, get it as polished as you can yourself.

Having decided to go this route, how do you find an editor? There are good editors and there are bad. The latter will take your money, and possibly keep taking your money as long as they can string you along. Treat an editor like a builder. A personal recommendation is the best reference.

You don't want a proof reader at this stage. A proof reader picks out typos and grammar errors. You are not looking for a copy editor either. The copy editor overlaps with the proof reader and will also check that you have your facts right. You want neither of those. What you want is a developmental editor or content editor. They are more or less the same thing.

There are many editors advertising online. You have no idea how good they are. I suggest joining an online writing community and asking them what editors they can recommend. If you get a personal recommendation from a writer, I suggest reading the book that has been edited. Is it any good? If it is, then that is a good reference. If not, I'd go for another editor.

Some editors offer a manuscript assessment. This is cheaper than a full edit and lets you know if your novel is good enough to make that worth it. Having done the assessment, the editor might say: yes, I can help you get this up to standard. Or they might say: sorry, I can't help you with this. They will give their reasons. Do take them seriously, but they are not the last word.

I found *writingtipsoasis.com*. There are 19 editors on this site, UK based, and each editor says something about themselves. I'd ask them for a reference that I could contact before taking them on. You could well be spending £1000 ($1200) or more, depending on the size of the book and how much work they have to do.

These days an editor needn't be in your country. But if you are working with them online, and they are elsewhere in the world, make double sure you check references. You won't be able to sue them if they are not much good, so check them out with other writers.

You could try an editor with the first chapter or two before going the whole hog and sending the full draft. And having to pay the hefty fee. That way, you'll know how they work, the effort they put in. And will be in a better position to assess them.

In brief, what you want to know from an editor is whether the draft is any good. You want them to be honest. You may be told the draft doesn't work and why, in full galling detail. Of course, that's their opinion and you could try elsewhere. You may be told that it's OK but needs work.

You want them to be specific: what works, what doesn't work, and what you can do about it.

If the draft is beyond editing...

If, say, three decent beta readers tell you this, forget employing an editor. Put your manuscript aside for at least six months. Then give it a read. Do you agree now that it doesn't work? I know you desperately want it to work, but try to see beyond that. If it doesn't work, then have done with it.

And write a new book.

My first book didn't work

An editor couldn't have helped me with it. It was beyond salvaging. A mess. After nine months of futility, I threw it in a corner and went to a writing class.

A few years later, as I have said above, I joined a local writers workshop (Newham Writers Workshop). If you attend one, and they discuss a piece that you have read to the group, you must listen. In fact, the best thing to do is shut up while they are assessing it, and not try to persuade the group that they have all misunderstood you.

I recall a particular writer who had been writing and rewriting the same novel for five years. He would bring a chapter into the writing workshop, and we would politely try to tell him it wasn't much good. He would be hurt and go off and rewrite. Over and over, he did this, and then bring it back again. All to no avail. It was one of these enterprises where the more you put into it, the more desperate you are for it to work. How else can you justify all that time and effort?

That writer couldn't be helped. He was fixed on a dream and didn't believe us. In the end, he stopped coming to the workshop. He might have gone to another one or given up writing. I have no ending to this tale.

What he should have done is given up on the book much earlier, and started another. Instead he went on writing, rewriting, and rewriting, until he must have been utterly sick of the work. But went on and on with it.

Let's suppose, on a more hopeful note, that yours is not too bad. Get down to it and rewrite where you need to. Make cuts where necessary. Don't be precious, which means holding on to a weak chapter because there's stuff you don't want to lose. Too bad. You have to toughen up.

After the rewrite

You go back to your beta reader, and hope they'll give you another go. Or you may have to try someone else if they are now too busy with their own writing.

What I do

I have developed as a writer in the school of hard knocks. I have had pieces accepted but have had lots of rejections too. As I continued writing, over the years, I became more self critical. I certainly wasn't to begin with, and held on to pieces I should have jettisoned. But I learnt the hard way. And that's what matters.

These days, I know that with a five week break, or longer, between first and second draft, I can be fairly confident at judging my manuscript. So it's only after the second draft that I involve my beta reader. She will read it, then suggest some changes, but usually nothing drastic. So far.

I can say no more, as we are talking about a book of yours that doesn't yet exist. Or if it does, I have no idea how good it might be. The best I can do is wish you luck with your drafts. And don't be despondent if a first book doesn't work.

Join the club, and have another go.

CHAPTER 18: Your Title

Your book has to have one. You can't keep calling it 'the book'. It's like a baby as yet unnamed, she needs one badly. A label that parents can refer to, can praise and play with, someone they call to on a crowded beach.

There are poets who call poems *Untitled*. Having been the editor of anthologies, when I get such a non-title title, in the contents I give the first line as the title, or part of it if it is a long line. Which means, in effect, I have titled it.

Titles are not copyrighted, but you can't piggy back on another's title. For example, if you wrote a book about a boarding school for magicians, you couldn't call it *Harry Potter and the Silver Candlestick*. J K Rowling will eat you for breakfast.

My favourite book title is: *On Grand Central Station I sat down and Wept* by Elizabeth Smart. It is not crime, but is so evocative. I can picture a young woman, sitting on a suitcase on the station concourse, weeping. It's long for a title, and usually titles are quite short. Very short, like *Gone Girl*. Though the two shortest I know are *M,* a German expressionist movie of 1931, with Peter Lorre as a child killer, directed by Fritz Lang. And *X* by Sue Grafton, one of her Alphabet series.

I tend to forget titles. I have read quite a number of Inspector Rebus novels, by Ian Rankin, but off the top of my head, I cannot think of one title. Does that matter? At the library or the bookshop, I am nudged by the blurbs to think I've read that but I don't recall that one.

Most of the crime novel titles I do remember have been films too, like *Murder on the Orient Express, Hound of the Baskervilles, Strangers on a Train, Brighton Rock, The Third Man.*

Here's some I do recall:

- *Murder Must Advertise* by Dorothy L Sayers
- *The Daughter of Time* by Josephine Tey
- *Farewell, My Lovely* by Raymond Chandler
- *The Maltese Falcon* by Dashiell Hammett
- *The Thirty-Nine Steps* by John Buchan
- *The Tiger in the Smoke* by Margery Allingham
- *The Postman Always Rings Twice* by James M. Cain

These are classics, all of them pre 1950s, which says a lot about me. I like film noir, which is 1940s, early 50s. Several of these have been filmed.

Titles can seem banal, like *The Third Man*. What's special about that? It is the quality of the writing and a brilliant film that makes it memorable. And then it is not banal at all.

Shakespeare has been mined, over and over, for titles. There are so many possibilities in his plays and sonnets. Mine away.

Titles in a Series

Sue Grafton has her Alphabet series of crime novels. It begins:

- *A is for Alibi*
- *B is for Burglar*

- *C is for Corpse*

- and ends: *Y is for Yesterday*

She died in 2017, before she could get to Z. In title terms, they are certainly memorable. *A is for Alibi* sticks in my head. Does it add difficulties to the author's task, if she begins with a title? It may do, but not necessarily, as restrictions can be helpful too. Your first page is slightly less blank.

Nicci French, the husband and wife partnership, use days of the week in the titles of their Frieda Klein series:

- *Blue Monday*

- *Tuesday's Gone*

- *Waiting for Wednesday*

- *Thursday's Children*

- *Friday on My Mind*

- *Saturday Requiem*

- *Sunday Morning Coming Down*

- *Day of the Dead*

Note the last one. Perhaps they were only planning a few, and never thought they'd get to seven. Or they didn't care if they did. They'd sort it out when and if they got there. Which they have, and it really doesn't matter that they've gone off piste.

My Series

From the first, my decision was to write a crime series. Not a single book, but an indeterminate number of books. Calling my main character Jack gave me the title of the first book,

Jack of All Trades. A builder, well, 'the House that Jack built', and all that, rang bells with me. At first I thought I'd make him a shoddy builder, but changed my mind fairly quickly once I got writing. But still kept the title for the first in the series. I then thought, why not *Jack something or other* for all the books. The series would be called after the title of the first book, the Jack of All Trades series.

The second book I called *Jack be Nimble*, and the third *Jack be Quick*. At which point I began to get confused. Which one was which? 'Nimble' and 'Quick' can be applied to just about any crime novel.

I decided the title had to say something about the novel, so I, at least, would know which was which. So the second had a name change and became *Jack of Spades,* where bodies are buried in Epping Forest, and the third became *Jack o'Lantern* where dirty work is done late at night. Soon after, I dropped the idea of restricting myself to well known phrases. Although there are plenty of Jack phrases, I had collected 120 in my title file, they didn't fit the brief in that they had to fit with the book. So I jettisoned the idea of using stock phrases, and decided I could make them up. There are two exceptions. *Jack by the Hedge* is the common name of a wild flower; I used that for the book set in a park. And *Jack in the Box* where Jack is a hostage in an armed siege.

The titles so far are:

- *Jack of All Trades*
- *Jack of Spades*
- *Jack o'Lantern*
- *Jack by the Hedge*
- *Jack in the Box*
- *Jack on the Tower*

- *Jack Recalled*

- *Jack at Death's Door*

- *Jack at the Gate*

Readers often can't remember which of the series they have read, but they do talk about Jack books. So do I in my newsletters. And I know which is which.

Working Title/Final Title

Authors often have a working title. One of mine was *Bike*. It was about a boy who desperately wants a bike. *Bike* would do for the time being, a label for the computer file. Not really for anyone else as I don't talk about work in progress, as I have found the more I speak about it, the less inclined I am to write it. So the working title is for me alone. Having finished the book, I knew a lot more about it, and came up with the final title, *Half a Bike*.

Summing Up

You must have a title for your book. It is a label for book-sellers, libraries and, of course, readers. The title may be soon forgotten by the reader, there are lots of books out there, but your name, hopefully, will be recalled if it was a good read.

EXERCISE 11

You are going to write a series of
crime novels with the same main
character and set in your area.
Come up with titles that connect in
some way for the first six novels.

CHAPTER 19:
Research I

I have referred to research in the chapter on main characters (Chapter 7). But research goes way beyond the main character. Almost every chapter could have had a research addendum. The research could be about the setting, other important characters, about lifestyle, clothing, pets, health, all aspects of human existence where our knowledge is thin.

Research is not simply checking an isolated fact. Well, OK, you might need to know the date of the first moon landing (20 July 1969). That's hardly research, just a simple question on Google which took me less than half a minute to look up. We can't call every single query 'research' or the term is meaningless. But if you need to know who the astronauts were, about the build up to the journey, the journey itself, what they did on the Moon, and the return to Earth, that's research.

One fact isn't, a hundred is. So our working definition for research is an investigation into an area of knowledge. The date of the moon landing could be the start of research, but it is not an investigation. How extensive the investigation will depend on your needs. If you have set your detective in Victorian London, then you'll need to do a lot of background reading, much more than I needed in finding out about Faraday cages (for *Jack at the Gate*) where an hour or so sufficed.

Why do research?

There are writers who feel they don't need research. Scorn the need for it. They've lived, they know enough. If they are, say, a lawyer or ex cop and are writing about their field of expertise, then maybe so. But I note John Grisham, who was a practising lawyer for around ten years, frequently thanks practitioners for their help in aspects of his novels.

Can't I just read crime novels and watch cop shows on TV?

You might get away with it if the subject is very domestic, or you may make glaring errors. I recall a member of the writers workshop I used to chair who read out a chapter of the novel he was writing which had several Muslim characters. An Asian English teacher present tore him to shreds as he had given them Hindu names. She was insulted that he had done so little research. A somewhat heavy evening at the writers group, but it was a reality check for him. I do recall his appalled expression at such a basic error. If he were to self publish, without that knowledge, he'd get painful reviews on Amazon. His mistake exposed. A copy editor could miss this too, if they don't know what they don't know.

Before I get too sanctimonious, I must make an admission. I've made a few errors in my published books. In one book, I had the police taking fingerprints with an ink pad and paper. Well, I had my fingerprints taken 30 years ago that way. I didn't realise things had changed, until a reviewer chastised me and told me they use digital scanners now.

That was bruising.

You may have to research an important character's work, especially if you are unfamiliar with it, be it plumbing or car mechanics. You need to know enough to make them believable.

You may have to research religion, say Roman Catholicism or Islam. There's plenty online and you can always ask a practitioner. I have considered having my builder work in a church. I am not religious so that would involve me finding out what work is done in church, by priests and by the various volunteers. I would have to go to church, to get the feel of the place and the people. I would also look for articles and books on the subject. I come in pretty green, so it would involve a fair amount of research.

You need to lift characters above the stereotype, be they gay, straight, black or white, trans or disabled. For example, you could have a private eye who also happens to be deaf. A fact of life which they have learned how to work with. But you'd need to know your stuff to make it credible.

Starters only

This is a brief chapter on research. It will be of little help if your book is set in, say, first century Rome, other than to say, don't overdo the research. There are bulging library shelves on the subject, tens of thousands of documents on the internet. You can easily get obsessive, bogged down in books and internet articles, and become so engrossed in the subject, terrified you might get some details wrong. Try not to, but don't forget you are not writing for university professors but for intelligent lay readers.

Which is not to say you mustn't do research to get the feel of the period. You will have to know about the rulers at the time, power struggles, beliefs and customs, clothing, food and other facts of everyday life. Read some books and various articles. Then get writing. As you write you will become aware of gaps in your knowledge. Make a note of them. When you finish the draft, research the areas you need now. And fix any errors in the next draft.

Police, the law and forensic science

How accurate does one need to be in portraying the police and their work? That's a moot question indeed. There are cops who won't watch cop shows on TV because they regard them as so full of errors on police procedure that they are unwatchable. I know a lawyer who refuses to watch trials on TV as they have him tearing his hair out for their abuse of the legal process.

A short while ago, I watched a TV cop show, *Vera,* a long running series. The lead cop is Detective Chief Inspector Vera Stanhope who works for the fictional Northumberland & City Police. It's a popular crime drama based on the books by crime writer Ann Cleeves. I won't blame Ann for the errors as she's not responsible for the TV adaptation. But if I noted errors, consider how irritated those in the field would be.

Vera and her sidekick walked into the crime scene, ducking under the police tape, to where a body lay, being photographed and examined. Well, they at least put on shoe covers before entering the crime scene. But that was the extent of their forensic awareness. In reality, they should be wearing full protective clothing, shoe covers, either a plastic or a paper suit with a hood, latex gloves and a face mask.

Why weren't they fully togged up? It's time consuming putting the gear on, but that's not the main reason. The protective clothing hides the actor's body and face. Wearing a face mask leaves only the eyes visible. The baggy suit is not figure flattering, an item not made to measure but coming in just a few standard sizes. Inevitably, as it is discarded after one visit to the crime scene. Actors are animated through body language and facial expression. Full protective clothing limits them so much; we hardly know who is who. Not good for TV or film. So they cheat.

I saw a similar carelessness in *Silent Witness*, a TV series about forensic pathologists! One of the pathologists was going round the crime scene in his everyday clothing, searching for samples of DNA etc. The more I look, the more I see. TV gets away with murder.

Not wearing full protective gear leads to possible contamination of the crime scene. A fibre of clothing, a hair or two left by an investigator which may not even be their own, ungloved hands can easily touch things with a slight stumble, and could thwart the investigation. Even walking with covered shoes is not recommended as any footprints made by the murderer, may be flattened. The CSIs (Crime Scene Investigators) lay a mat-path to protect the ground.

But here's the point, I am not a cop and I wasn't all that bothered in either show. I shrugged it off and continued watching. I spotted the errors of procedure because I write crime novels and have read up about crime scenes for this book. Most viewers wouldn't have turned a hair. I dare say, the director and their technical experts knew exactly what they were doing. They knew it was no way to treat a crime scene. But they made a calculation, something like this: less than 1% of our viewers are cops and forensic professionals, so let's forget them. We'll never satisfy them whatever we do.

Crime writers often make the same calculation. At least, subconsciously. A real detective, given a red pen and a crime book, would deface a police procedural with crossings out. It's not just crime scene malpractice; murder investigations are team efforts, not simply the star cop swanning it and taking all the glory.

There's truth, and there's fiction. We write fiction. So we have license. Although we can't be totally truthful, we should aim to minimise errors, not simply because cops may be reading, but the general public are becoming more knowledgeable.

Police Ranks

You may be writing a police procedural or you may have a private eye as your sleuth. Either way, when there's a murder the cops are called in. You need to know who is who.

Detectives in the police force are plain clothes cops, usually in suits, but certainly not flamboyantly dressed. There are, of course, uniformed police, but in general they play peripheral roles in our crime novels as our writing is centred on detection.

The ranks of the detective in the UK, in ascending order, are (abbreviations in brackets):

- Detective Constable (DC)

- Detective Sergeant (DS)

- Detective Inspector (DI)

- Detective Chief Inspector (DCI)

- Detective Superintendent (D/Supt)

Beyond those ranks, the appellation 'Detective' is no longer used. Remove the term 'Detective' from the above and you have the uniform ranks. There is often a family liaison officer (FLO), a constable, whose role is to assist the family of a murder victim. Being close to the family they may pick up responses or clues important to the investigation.

The higher ranks are:

- Chief Superintendent

- Deputy Commander

- Commander

- Deputy Chief Constable (Deputy Commissioner in the Metropolitan Police)

- Chief Constable (Commissioner in the Met)

A Murder Investigation Team (MIT) is led by a Senior Investigating Officer (SIO). SIOs are of D/Supt rank, or above if it is a high profile case and/or there are multiple murders.

Police in the UK don't carry guns, but armed response can be called if it is felt to be necessary.

Comparison with the US

The US police ranks are more like the military than UK police. They carry guns. The murder rate is 30 times higher in the US than the UK, where 36% of the US population own guns.

The US ranks vary somewhat across the various states and major cities, but commonly they are:

- Police technician

- Police officer, patrol officer, police detective

- Police corporal

- Police sergeant

- Police lieutenant

- Police captain

- Deputy police chief

- Chief of police or Commissioner or Sheriff

- Some police departments have colonel and major ranks too.

A police technician is entry level, a rookie doing support work, like a trainee police constable in the UK. We don't have a corporal in the UK, so a police sergeant is slightly higher than a sergeant in the UK. But this is a rough and ready comparison, as it depends on the area they are policing, whether rural or metropolitan, and the population size. A police lieutenant is roughly Inspector level. A police captain corresponds to Superintendent or Chief Superintendent.

A Murder Scene

Let's consider how a police investigation gets going. It could begin with a 999 call. At that point it may not be clear there is a murder. The first at the scene might be a police constable. Once they realise there has been a murder, or possible murder, they will phone the station and allow no one in or out of the crime scene. They may be able to do some preliminary questioning, but will take care not to contaminate the site in any way.

A detective inspector might be on call at the station or at home. They will rush to the scene with full 'blues and twos' (blue for the flashing light, two for the two tone siren) as the first hour, known as the 'golden hour', is the richest time for evidence retrieval. The detective will have with them, as routine, a murder bag containing such items as protective clothing and a torch.

Arriving quickly, too, would be the Crime Scene Investigators (CSI), sometimes called Scene of Crime Officers (SOCO). I'll stick with the better known CSI. CSI will put police tape around the area, and begin to investigate the scene. All investigators will be in protective clothing.

Uniformed officers will arrive and will be utilised to keep the public away and to guard the crime scene. One of them will be in charge of the crime scene book which details who comes and goes in the area, and making sure all are correctly attired. If the crime scene is in the open air, a large tent will be erected over the corpse and some of the scene. In charge of the CSI team is the Crime Scene Manager, with responsibility to collect as much forensic material as possible.

A forensic pathologist may arrive about this time to do an investigation of the body in situ. The pathologist will give a first response to the detectives. It may be obvious how the person was killed, say a knifing or a shooting, but may not be. We may have a suicide, yet to be ascertained. All the more need for care. The coroner's office must be notified to move the body for an autopsy (post mortem). They will send an officer to the crime scene.

CSI will continue working on site until they believe there is nothing forensically useful to be found. Depending on the complexity of the crime scene, they may be there a few days or a few weeks.

Police Jargon and Abbreviations

Some writers go in for these in a big way, for authenticity. My feeling is to be helpful, and to expect that your reader dips into crime, rather than they are a total aficionado. They may puzzle whether a DS is a Detective Sergeant or Detective Superintendent. It is the former, several rungs lower in the hierarchy; the latter is D/Supt. Why should the general reader know this?

Every so often, I suggest writing a police rank in full. And ditto with such pieces of police jargon as: perp (perpet-rator), misper (missing person). A UCO is an undercover officer, an OCG is an organised crime group (or gang). An FLO is a family liaison officer, to keep the victim's family in touch with developments. The rule for abbreviations is to use them as little as possible. We are writing for the general reader, not the police force.

An acronym you may come across is HOLMES, the UK police computer program. It stands for Home Office Large Major Enquiry System. HOLMES is used to connect major crimes across the UK. So for instance, if a suspect is arrested in Scotland, the police will know he was arrested for a similar crime in Cornwall two years previously. Don't just throw it in without explanation. Though you will need a little subtlety if you have, say, two police detectives talking to each other. They have no need to explain what HOLMES is to each other, but you don't want a puzzled reader.

You could try something like this:

'Do a search on HOLMES.'

'I'd best try her single and her married name.' He tapped a few keys. 'Got her. Can't beat HOLMES for up to date info. Photo and full details. Take a look, sir.' He backed away from the screen.

Such head to heads are not uncommon, two experts talking to each other. They don't need to explain their jargon but you, the writer, do. However you do it, don't make it obvious.

Forensic Science

Often shortened to forensics, this utilises the scientific method and processes to obtain evidence which could be used in court.

Forensics has become increasingly sophisticated and covers such areas as fingerprinting, DNA, blood splatter analysis, fibre analysis, pollen analysis, entomology and ballistics.

I shall say a little more about fingerprinting and DNA, and merely give some pointers about the others. My purpose is to give an indication of what you might need as this is primarily a book on writing. Not on the details of forensics.

Areas of Forensics

Blood splatter analysis is used at a messy scene where, say, the victim has been hit over the head with a hammer and there is intense splatter on the walls, bedding and carpet. The extent of splatter will give clues on the blood pattern likely to be on the murderer's clothing, and the murder weapon.

Fibre analysis, say of a single fibre found at the scene, could tell what make of coat the murderer was wearing. Or he/she might have brought a fibre from their home, on clothing or shoes, from a cushion or carpet, and left it at the scene inadvertently.

Pollen analysis could be used on a suspect's shoes when examining the mud on the soles. Such analysis might tell whether a suspect had been to the field where certain flowers were in bloom, and the victim was found.

Entomology is the study of insects, and is most useful in forensics when a body has been dead for some time. It is essential to get a date, as close as possible, to the act of murder. Flies lay eggs in a decaying corpse, and a study of the larvae and adult flies can give an indication of date to an expert.

Ballistics is the study of guns and bullets. A particular gun will make unique scratches on a bullet, of evidential value where there has been a shooting. The gun may have been used in other killings.

Fingerprints

Fingerprints are utterly distinctive to the individual. They are most useful when there are clear impressions. Often prints are smudged or partial. In such cases, whether they belong to a defendant in a court case is a source of argument by experts on both sides. Though good prints can be damning.

At the crime scene, CSI will always search for fingerprints as they are such good evidence. Some prints may be obvious, say on a window pane, or in a blood mark. Others are latent, which means they are not visible. Some show up in ultraviolet light. The police have chemicals too which can bring out fingerprints. Surfaces may be dusted with fine powder which then shows up any prints.

Once a fingerprint is revealed, it is photographed, and then adhesive tape is placed over it to pick it off the surface. The tape is stuck onto white card. The tape on the card (with the print) is known as a 'last'. The photographs and lasts are sent off to a fingerprint officer. They will judge whether a print is distinctive enough and if so, will scan it into their database which has millions of fingerprints on it from those with a criminal record.

Anyone who may have been at the crime scene will have their fingerprints taken, whether they are a suspect or not. The obviously innocent have theirs taken for elimination purposes. These will be destroyed after the investigation.

Fingerprints used to be taken with an ink pad and paper which had spaces for each finger of each hand. Nowadays, scanners are used. They are cleaner, and the prints go straight into the database, making it easier to find a potential match.

DNA

This is short for deoxyribonucleic acid, and is contained in every cell of your body. Your DNA is unique to you. The only exception is identical twins (or identical triplets etc). Such twins come from an egg which splits in half in their mother's womb, and each half matures. There have been cases involving twins, where DNA evidence was insufficient as it cannot say which of the two was at the scene. Other evidence must be introduced to secure a conviction, such as fingerprints. Not even twins duplicate these.

DNA detection has become increasingly sophisticated. Just a few skin cells can be enough. But, with such sensitivity, contamination becomes an important factor, which is why investigators at the scene must wear protective clothing. And bag and label any material straight away. Labs too must take precautions against cross contamination. Carelessness can lead to wrongful convictions.

Where there is DNA evidence, anyone involved, in however a small way, will have to give a DNA sample. This is usually done by taking a scraping of the inside cheek with a small swab. The swab is put in a small bottle, labelled as to whose sample it is, who took it and when. All this must be done in a sterile manner, using latex gloves, sterile swab and bottle.

CCTV

There are CCTV cameras in thousands of places around the country. In shops, streets, stations, banks, pubs, even parks. The images can be vital in showing that a suspect was in the area at a certain time. Or even at the scene itself. They can though be of poor quality, especially if the light is bad, and are then of marginal use.

ANPR (Automatic Number Plate Recognition)

There are cameras on major roads up and down the country which read number plates of vehicles that pass. Evidence that a particular car has been at a place at a certain time may be important evidence in a case.

Digital Analysis

This area has become increasingly important as more and more people communicate with mobile phones, laptops, tablets, and desktop computers. Experts will take these away from suspects, along with those that belonged to the victim, to have them forensically examined. A lot of information can be gleaned from emails, texts, Facebook communications, and phone calls. Who has been talking to whom about what may prove vital. Such communications can tell of affairs, plans afoot with co-conspirators, drug deals etc. While spoken phone calls are not available, voicemail messages are, and a list of phone calls could show that a suspect has been in regular contact with, say, the victim, when they have denied such contact.

A murderer may attempt to delete information on phones and computers, but this is often retrievable by experts.

The Autopsy

This is also known as a post mortem. It is a surgical examination of a dead body, usually at a mortuary, carried out by a forensic pathologist, who may have gone to the crime scene or more usually that first inspection will be carried out by CSI. CSI at the crime scene will contact the coroner's office. And once given authorisation, they will prepare the body for transportation to the mortuary.

The purpose of the autopsy is to determine the cause and manner of death. They will also give information on such matters as whether a victim was raped, whether a woman was pregnant, any diseases the victim had, whether they were a drug user and so forth.

A forensic pathologist will examine the body externally and internally.

Violent deaths come in various guises: shootings, knifing, drownings, strangulations, hangings, blunt instrument, extreme battering, poisoning, gassing. Such a death could be accidental, a suicide or inflicted by another person. For suspected poisoning, organs such as liver, heart and stomach contents will be removed for chemical analysis.

The forensic pathologist will attempt to ascertain the time of death as accurately as possible. The more recent the death, the more accurate this can be. How far rigor mortis, stiffening of the body, has progressed will tie down the time of death somewhat. This begins to set in after three or four hours, and after twelve the body can be completely rigid. The pathologist will take the rectal temperature, which cools after death, the extent is a guide to time of death, but the cooling is dependent on body weight and ambient temperature.

The exact time of death is a complex, much studied area. If the body is discovered months after death, then other experts will have to be brought in, such as entomologists. The date of such a death ascertained may only be accurate to within a week or so.

Following the autopsy there will be an inquest. This will be adjourned if a murder investigation is underway, and concluded when it is completed.

The Crown Prosecution Service (CPS) in the UK decides whether there is sufficient evidence to put a suspect on trial for murder. In the US, this is the role of the district attorney's office. The pathologist will be an important witness for the prosecution. Their report is made available to the defence as well as the prosecution. At the trial they will be cross examined by the defence barrister whose job it is to emphasise areas of doubt.

The same applies to other forensic witnesses. The defence may decide to employ their own experts, say for a smudged fingerprint where experts on both sides argue its validity.

CHAPTER 20:
Research II

Back at the Station

Once it is believed that a murder has been committed, then a Major Incident Team (MIT) will be assembled. In charge will be the Senior Investigating Officer (SIO). The MIT will work from an incident room in one of the larger police stations. There can be 50 or more in the team, including detectives, uniform, CSI and other forensic investigators.

In the incident room will be desks with a battery of computers, and a few large screens for displays at team meetings. Meetings may be daily, especially in the early days as discoveries can come in thick and fast. Team members need to be up to date or they will do unnecessary work.

Large investigations inevitably break up into smaller teams, say for going house to house, searching woodland, questioning suspects at the police station, and forensic areas. Other experts may be drawn in as necessary.

Being Arrested

Initially, witnesses and suspects may be questioned at their home or place of work. Important witnesses will be required to come into the station to give a full statement. This is not an arrest. A suspect will only be arrested if there is a belief that they may be the perpetrator of the crime.

On arrest, they are given a warning in this form:

You are under arrest on suspicion of [offence]. You do not have to say anything, but it may harm your defence if you do not mention when questioned something which you later rely on in court. Anything you do say may be given in evidence.

They will be taken to the police station for questioning. At this point they have not been charged. It is important to note the difference between being held for questioning and being charged. Members of the public, and the media too, often get this wrong, causing suffering to someone later released without charge, whose life has been turned upside down in the sensational press.

Arrested persons have the right to inform someone of their arrest, though this can be delayed if it is felt this will harm the investigation. They have the right to consult a solicitor. The suspect will be photographed, have fingerprints and their DNA taken. There's no choice in this. There are, though, strict rules for how long a person can be held without charge. They are detailed in the Police and Criminal Evidence Act (PACE).

A suspect can be detained for up to 24 hours initially. If more time is needed for questioning, a senior officer, Chief Superintendent and above, can grant another 12 hours. More than that, and the suspect has to be taken before a magistrate's court for extra time to be granted. The maximum time a suspect can be held, without charge, is 96 hours. This length of time is rare. Either the suspect will be released without charge, or will be charged.

Police Questioning of Suspects

This will be done in a room specific for this purpose. It will be a bare room, without any distracting posters, with the only furniture a table and chairs. For murder, the interview is likely to be videoed so there is both a recording of the questions and the answers and visual behaviour. It protects the suspect from threats and harassment during the interview. An arrested person will be entitled to consult their solicitor before questioning begins.

At the beginning of the interview, those present will introduce themselves. The main interviewer, for a murder case, will be of detective sergeant rank or above.

And then the questioning will begin. At one extreme, the suspect may say 'no comment' to every question. No matter what evidence is shown to them. This could be a short interview. At the other extreme, once shown damning evidence, they may confess to the crime. This must be heard without any coercion, or it will not be acceptable in court.

The interview will be watched by other detectives as it is happening, either by video or through one-way glass. If there is a court case, the interview will inevitably be important evidence to be put before the jury.

Whether to go to Trial

In the UK, this will be ascertained by the Crown Prosecution Service. They need to believe that the gathered evidence and interviews are sufficient for a reasonable chance of conviction.

Murder trials are held at Crown Courts. A judge is in charge and there are 12 people on the jury who ultimately decide on the guilt or innocence of the defendant.

EXERCISE 12

Two detectives are questioning a suspect. The suspect has been held for questioning but not yet charged. The detectives believe the suspect did it. The suspect has a lawyer present.

Begin with introductions. What are the detective ranks? Write 500 words from one of the detectives' point of view as the interview proceeds. The detectives have a good item of evidence. Hold it back, but use it. How will the suspect react?

CHAPTER 21: Research I did for *Jack of All Trades*

Police and Legal

Before I began writing this series, my knowledge of how the police investigated a murder was limited to what I'd picked up from crime novels, TV and films. Though I had been on two juries in Crown Courts, my thinking was vague as I'd had no necessity to use it in writing.

I wasn't sure of the police ranks. I had to look them up once I needed to bring in the cops. In the first book, *Jack of All Trades*, there is a murder in a large house in Chigwell where Jack is working. The police are called. I needed to know the way the police work. How they interview witnesses and suspects, the protective clothing worn at a crime scene, evidence gathering etc.

I had to research questioning at the police station. There's plenty online to help with this. I watched TV shows with more awareness, with a "need to know" eye, especially true crime, where police and lawyers are shown as they actually work.

I had to use the police caution in the novel: the form of words the police use on arresting someone. I needed to bear in mind the difference between being arrested under suspicion, where a suspect can be held for up to four days then must be released, and being charged with murder. A major difference, of course, but it may not feel like it for the suspect who wonders whether they'll ever be released.

The above knowledge was sufficient for the first book. I needed more as the series progressed. But one book at a time. You needn't overburden yourself.

Jack's Work

This was an area of research I had not anticipated. Naive of me, you might say. And I agree. I had selected a builder as my main character as he works in different places, giving me lots of settings for murders. But a builder's work is skilled, and I am not a builder. So I had to research the work he does. I became quite envious of Charlaine Harris with her cleaner, Lily Bard, in Shakespeare, Arkansas. I am quite familiar with a vacuum cleaner and sponge.

I bought some second hand books on DIY which have proved useful for ladders, tools, materials etc, and for various areas of work like bricklaying and plumbing. A very good source is YouTube where there are videos of builders working, informing viewers about their materials and exactly what they are doing. I thank them all for their expertise in such matters, which I have used throughout the series.

As my main character is a builder, I have to ensure the reader believes this. He works, he interacts with people in the setting, he goes to get materials. On YouTube I watched videos on erecting a scaffolding tower, bricklaying, using a mini digger, making a soundproof walls, constructing a concrete parking area, pointing brickwork and roof repairs.

I didn't need all that at once. One job per book. That's enough, thank you very much. In the first, Jack is working on a summerhouse. This is not simply a large shed, but has a bedroom, a sitting room, a small kitchen and bathroom.

The summerhouse is in the grounds of a multi-millionaire's premises. Jack is there to change windows for a new design and renew the floorboards.

Nothing especially tricky there. Though I had to look up dry rot. Later in the book, Jack is sent off to put a new front door on a flat. I looked up how he might do this single-handed with a heavy door.

The Settings

There are two settings in the first novel in the series. The first is where Jack lives in Forest Gate, East London. Well, I live there too and I imagined him living up my road. No research needed in this book, but it was necessary in others: I had an armed siege in a house, action in nearby West Ham Park in another, and one novel set at the local cemetery. Each of which are places I could walk to and take notes.

The other setting in the first novel is where Jack is working. I needed a large millionaire's house. I had once visited such a house in Chigwell. OK, I thought, Chigwell will do. I looked up estate agents online for Chigwell, and I came up with Manor Road. I looked at it on Google Earth and saw large, expensive houses. I visited the area to get the feel of the street and the houses. I walked up and down it several times. With my notebook, it was fortunate I wasn't pulled up by the police for casing the area.

Would they believe me that I was doing research for a book?

Using a road map, I worked out how Jack might drive there from Forest Gate.

Other Research for the First Novel

Jack is a recovering alcoholic. I read several books on this. A friend of mine was going to a recovery group nearby. I questioned him on how the group worked and came up with Alcohol Halt, a group that Jack goes to several times in the book.

Jack's hobby is astronomy. It's an area I am interested in too. So that suited me. I decided that he had a telescope. The major problem in a city for stargazers is light pollution. So I decided that Jack would go to an area on the edge of Epping Forest on clear dark nights. After the first book, I decided I would keep him more local for his astronomical forays. And sent him out on Wanstead Flats, a nearby area of football pitches and scrubland.

I needed to know more about the inside of the house where the millionaire couple lived. Although Jack is working outside, he comes in from time to time. I also switched viewpoints in the novel, one of whom was Joanna's, the lady of the house. I had to know about the sitting room, the kitchen and the upstairs rooms. An important scene is a party at the house, where Jack feels quite out of place. The guests are in the long sitting room, the French windows wide open so that guests can spill out onto the lawn, where a quartet is playing classical music in front of the summerhouse.

Online estate agents often have video tours of big houses. I did a few to get the feel of such places.

At the party, the men wore suits. Simple enough. But women have a variety of wear for smart occasions. Not my expertise at all. I researched various outfits from magazines with a fashion section.

Research isn't difficult. The internet has made it a lot easier for writers. So there's no excuse for not doing it. Leave it out and your book will appear thin and will inevitably have mistakes. Do it and your characters and settings will be richer.

CHAPTER 22: Ready, Steady, Go

I have covered types of crime novels, possible main char-acters, sidekicks and other characters, settings and research as well as the writing topics. The latter will apply to other novels too, but I have kept crime novels to the fore. You may be writing a single book or going for a series. Though you may begin with a one-off and then decide to write another with the same main characters. Many writers have gone that way, and a series has developed. Others, like myself, decided from the beginning that they were going to write a series. And selected a main character and an area to make that possible.

It's now over to you. Begin with your notes for your book. Develop your main character, think about the setting, and if it is real then walk the streets. Think about the other characters. You want conflict between the characters. Families are good, especially those getting on badly. Write it up. Do your preliminary research.

And, when you think you have enough, begin writing your novel. A first line, a first paragraph, a first page. You must settle on the viewpoint: first person or third? If unsure, go for third person. You could write a first chapter, and reassess.

Once I start the novel, I write every day. I might have a weekend off, though it's not really off as I will likely write some notes or certainly be thinking about my story.

It may be tricky to write every day if you have commitments, such as a young family, but I think it is necessary. Writing occasionally won't work. It's OK for short stories but not a novel. A novel needs the fire of invention. If you don't keep feeding it, the fire will go out. And once it is out you may not be able to light it again.

When I can maintain a good glow, I know the book is working. I am thinking about it all the time, thinking of possibilities, alternatives. I can envisage the characters, and the writing flows.

If I don't feel the heat, especially after I have written several chapters, then I stop. I need to examine why. Something has gone wrong. Unless I can sort out what, there's no point going on. You might call it intuition, but I don't feel it is that. It is experience. I have been writing for more than three decades and have learnt from my winners and losers along the way.

But if you are a beginner, how can you detect when a book is not working? Can you feel the characters? Can you see where the story is going? A tip I gave early on is worth repeating. If unsure whether your novel is working at any point, stop. And interview the characters. I mean in writing. Ask them what they are thinking, what is bothering them? Let the interview flow. Hopefully, they will develop as you gather their motivation and learn more about them.

And here I leave you. Your book is your book. Only you can write it, and at a certain point you must begin. Or you will forever wonder if you ever could be a writer. Remember the trinity: character, story, language. Keep it tight!

I hope I'll be reading you soon.

Appendix

APPENDIX 1: Reading and Research for This Book

Inevitably writers learn from other writers. I picked up the tricks of the trade for crime writing from myriad writers of the genre. Some are listed in this appendix. For the writing chapters, I looked over my teaching notes.

I attended a playwriting course at the City Lit in the early 70s, the tutor was Cathy Itzen whose enthusiasm got my first play on the move. I attended a novel and short story course at the same institution in the 1980s, with tutor Carol Burns, where I began to get the hang of point of view. I attended Newham Writers Workshop from 1988 to 2013 and value the friendship and supportive criticism I received there.

For fact checking, I used Wikipedia extensively. I give them a little money each year as they are a valuable resource. I darted here and there on the internet for the odd quote and more extensive facts, such as the ranks of US cops.

I read a few books to fill in my gaps:

- *Forensics* by Val McDermid, Profile Books 2015

- *The Crime Writer's Casebook* by Stephen Wade and Stuart Gibbon, Straightforward Publishing 2018

- *Plotting and Writing Suspense Fiction* by Patricia Highsmith, Poplar Press 1983
- *The Craft of Novel-Writing* by Dianne Doubtfire, Alison & Busby 1978

APPENDIX 2: Some Crime Writers I Have Enjoyed

I am an impatient reader; I need to be gripped by a novel within the first 20 pages. What keeps me reading are interesting characters, ongoing conflict, use of setting and quality of language. Most crime books I read, I take out from the local library. A third of them I don't finish, the prime reason being I don't care about the characters.

These books, read in the last five years, I rate as 5 star reads (out of 5). I have allowed only one novel per writer, although for quite a few of these authors I have read more.

A Private Business	Barbara Nadel
After the Fire	Henning Mankell
All Day and a Night	Alafair Burke
Another One Goes Tonight	Peter Lovesey
As Time Goes By	Mary Higgins Clark
The Bird Watcher	William Shaw
Blood Salt Water	Denise Mina
Brat Farrar	Josephine Tey

Brush Back	Sara Paretsky
The Burglar who Counted the Spoons	Lawrence Block
Career of Evil	Robert Galbraith
The Cellar	Minette Walters
Day of the Dead	Nicci French
Don't Let Go	Harlan Coben
Far From True	Linwood Barclay
Fleshmarket Close	Ian Rankin
Harbour Street	Ann Cleeves
Hidden Killers	Lynda La Plante
The Keys to the Street	Ruth Rendell
The Kill	Jane Casey
Kind of Cruel	Sophie Hannah
Little Boy Blue	MJ Arlidge
The Long Way Home	Louise Penny
Love You Dead	Peter James
The Murder Room	PD James
Post Mortem	Kate London
Rain Dogs	Adrian McKinty
The Red House	Emily Winslow
Rogue Lawyer	John Grisham
Splinter the Silence	Val McDermid
Stamboul Train	Graham Greene
The Strange Disappearance of a Bollywood Star	Vaseem Khan

The Talented Mr Ripley	Patricia Highsmith
The Trespasser	Tana French
Whose Body?	Dorothy L Sayers
The Word is Murder	Anthony Horowitz
The Zig Zag Girl	Elly Griffiths

APPENDIX 3: My Answers to the Exercises

EXERCISE 1

I started my novel with Jim Price in a difficult situation, namely: waking up in a bed, in a strange room, next to a naked, dead woman.

Invent a difficult situation for your main character. Just a few sentences will do. Beginning with that situation, write the next 500 words.

My Answer

Having written the exercise, I recalled I had done the same thing before in another novel of mine, *Hell's Chimney*. I have a young man tied up in the dark. That was all I knew before I began. I had to come up with reasons which I did as I went along. Here's the first 500 words.

The darkness was total. Not a chink of light, no indication of walls or ceiling. No window. Straw was under his puffed up hands, tied too tightly behind his back. He could feel the blueness, the pins and needles in the fingers as he tried to move them in the damp straw. His ankles too were bound. Was he in a barn? The urine from a horse, or was it his own? He groaned and rolled in a sea of pain: bloated hands, ankles, his right eye throbbed, flashing deep redness. The side of his face ached. Patches of his body cried out their bruising.

He remembered the kicking. They'd grabbed him, he had struggled – and they came in punching with fists and boots. He'd tried to protect his head with his hands but they'd ripped his arms away. They trod on his fingers and they went for his helplessness. He'd screamed and yelled for his mother, of all people. Dead three years. Mother to come and stop them, to rip them away. To save him, to make it stop.

The thought brought tears. Perhaps for his mother, but mainly for his sorry self, trussed like a chicken, kicked into unconsciousness. He tugged at his wrist bonds. There was no give. The circulation must be almost cut off; he could lose his hands. He tried wriggling the fingers and groaned as if they were still kicking him.

Toby was on his side, his ear and cheek in the pungent straw. How long before they come? They must come soon. Was this simply a lesson? He had stormed out of his father's presence declaring he could never respect that woman. That woman, who had bewitched his father and now insisted on replacing his mother. 'Call me Mother,' she had declared. And he yelled, 'I'll call you bitch.'

Fool. There are things which must not be said. It was the drink. And the sight of Zeke, her crow ugly son, loving it as his own father dressed him down. And she, sweet loveliness herself. The bitch. She had his father on a string. She pulled and father yelled and screamed and ranted at him. It was like a pummelling with hot coals, with the lady nodding, smiling reassurance while father harangued.

Until he broke.

He had thrown his plate at her. The chicken flopped into her lap. Onion and gravy besmirched her face and her yellow dress. She was not smiling then. Her lips pressed thin, her eyes blazing at him. Oh no, she was not smiling then.

He must apologise. Eat crow, lick boots. How it had all burst out of him! Wine words, wine insults - and on top of it - throwing the plate. This was the result. Beaten up, tied up in this stink hole. He groaned and rolled, wanting to rub his jaw, scratch his ribs. He yanked

himself to sitting position but it was no
better. The ache and pain moved round him
as he moved. From jaw to belly, to ribs,
to hands.

EXERCISE 2

List 5 crime novels you have
read. Say whether they are cozy,
hard boiled or in-between. Which
of the categories below best fits
each one?

- Police Procedural
- Police Associates
- Private Eyes (amateur or pro-
  fessional?)
- Workers
- Accidental detective
- Historical
- Killers

My Answer

- *The Talented Mr Ripley* by Patricia Highsmith [Killers, In-between]

- *The Trespasser* by Tana French [Police procedural, Hard boiled]

- *The Word is Murder* by Anthony Horowitz [Private Eye – professional, In-between]

- *Day of the Dead* by Nicci French [Police Associates, Hard boiled]

- *The Long Way Home* by Louise Penny [Police Procedural, In-between]

EXERCISE 3

What is a story? Write your answer in one sentence.

I gave my answer a little later in the chapter. It is the only exercise that I set mid chapter as the question is rather a teaser. So simple, and yet not so simple. We recognise a story, but it isn't obvious what it actually is.

My Answer

- A story is about a character with a problem that is in some way resolved.

EXERCISE 4

Your character is a killer. He has three people to kill. Come up with a reason why.

He sets off to kill the first one. Write 500 words from your killer's viewpoint.

My Answer

Call me Nick. I am a loyal citizen. Not of your country. I won't say which, then you won't have to be silenced. Don't worry, that's a joke. I work in the Embassy. Nominally in tourism. I know a lot about your country. I travel all over the place. I keep up the website for our citizens. I am never critical, I only say good things. I like Shakespeare and the

Queen. I enjoy a pint of real ale. I have read all of Jane Austen. I've been to Dove Cottage several times and to the Brontë Parsonage in Haworth. It rained all the time, but that's to be expected in Yorkshire.

I take my tourist work seriously. I must be known as the tourism officer by all who matter. I get free tickets, I am invited to museums and to festivals. All very nice. It's excellent cover for my real activity.

I kill the enemies of my country. Here, in your country. I do not stand in judgement. I leave that to my superiors. They know all the facts. I am simply a soldier if you will. I do my duty.

I have different ways of operating. This is important. If I always killed in the same way, the pattern would be noticed. That wouldn't necessarily mean I'd be caught but it would create a fuss. And I must minimise fuss.

I sent a car over a cliff. Two occupants, very sad, except they were traitors. The inquest said it was an accident. I use poison too, but only for individuals. It would be stupid to poison a whole family as that would ensure forensic investigation. No, individuals only. My poison of choice causes heart attack. Excellent means for middle aged or elderly targets. No questions asked.

I have a wife and three children. My wife used to work in the Embassy in the trade department. She does a little freelance work for her old department from time to time, but our home in Harrow and the children keep her busy. Two of the children are at an independent school near our home. And the youngest starts pre-prep next year. I like your independent schools, but your state schools are inferior.

My wife knows I must travel in my job. I don't have a mistress, if that's what you are thinking. I don't approve of such things. A man should look after his family, be loyal and expect loyalty in return. It means I can go back to a quiet home where there is no stress. Where I will not be betrayed. Not that my wife knows anything of my activities beyond my tourism role. That is as it should be.

I receive my assignments in code, one every three months on average. It doesn't appear to be coded, but rather it seems to be a tourist document. Within it, there are numbers. They look like phone numbers or map references, but in actuality they refer to lines on the page, then a word in that line, then a letter. It is quite arduous, the decoding. I do it at home, upstairs in my office. I have to check and recheck. I must be absolutely sure of my instructions.

I am a little bothered by my current assignment. I trust my superiors implicitly. My role is to take out traitors. To be a deterrent. This job though has me wondering. I have to kill a family. The husband, the wife and a teenage daughter. I can fully understand the husband and the wife. Whatever it is, they are in it together. But a thirteen year old girl?

My own daughter is 13. The girl cannot
have done anything.

I wonder whether to just kill the
parents. Let the girl go. Like Snow
White. You see why I am telling you this?

EXERCISE 5

Imagine you are using your local
area as the setting for your crime
novel. Write down:

a) 10 places in your area where
your main character might go

b) two people who might be in each
location. Say what they are doing.

My Answer

I live in Forest Gate, in the East End of London. Ten local
places with two people doing something are:

- *The Forest Tavern:* A young man on a stool is talking to
the barmaid who is pulling him a pint of beer.

- *Forest Gate Library:* Two teenage girls, who should be doing homework, are at a table with books spread out, looking at one of their phones and laughing.

- *Forest Gate Station:* A uniformed policewoman is talking to a teenage boy in school uniform. The boy is looking very sheepish as he has been caught trying to dodge his fare.

- *Familia Cafe:* A man and a woman in their 30s are at a table by the window. They are holding hands under the table. She is looking out of the window nervously.

- *The Co-op Supermarket*: A young woman is running out of the shop with a box of chocolates. Two of the staff are after her. They catch her fifty yards away where two men are waiting for her.

- *Forest Gate Community Garden:* An elderly man and a teenage boy are at a table with compost and pots. They are potting up iris rhizomes.

- *Durning Hall Community Centre*: Two teenage girls wearing white martial arts gear are at the reception counter. One of them has had her phone stolen.

- *The Methodist Church*: There is a jumble sale. A young woman is haggling with the woman at the table over a blouse. She has spotted the designer label.

- *Wanstead Flats:* A man at the edge of a football pitch is yelling at the young woman refereeing the match, calling her a blind cow.

- *The Cemetery:* An elderly woman is weeding a grave. There are fresh lilies in an urn. A young woman with her is texting on her phone.

EXERCISE 6

Take a character of yours and interview them. This is a useful technique for finding out more about them, akin to the way actors work in exploring a character.

If you don't have a character, then interview the baddy in a fairy story, say the wolf or the giant. A baddy will not likely admit they are bad. They will lie to you. Alternatively, they could boast of their wickedness.

My Answer

I did this interview for Alison Bell, Jack's ex-wife, as I was in the middle of writing *Jack on the Tower*. I was having a bit of trouble, so I interviewed all the main characters, and it got me on the move again.

• *Why have you kept the surname Bell?*

It's my daughter's name. She was born when I was married to Jack Bell. Everyone at school knew me as Mrs Bell, and I've just kept the name. I don't want to revert to my single name, I mean I might get married again, and I can't keep changing my name, not as a professional person.

• *How do you like your new school, Alison?*

I don't. It might prove a mistake, leaving Brighton. I don't feel well supported. My deputy is useless. I don't know how she got the job. She's obviously resentful that I got the head's job and she didn't. There are quite a few weak teachers but I can't come in like a hurricane. I have to win trust. And there could be an Ofsted inspection anytime. The trouble is when you have a poor school, the good people leave and you are left with the weaker ones. I did it myself. Judged the school each time and moved on to suit myself. Now I can't. I have to improve the school.

• *What's the journey to school like?*

If the traffic's not bad, I can do it in 15 minutes. Though it took me an hour the other day. Such a waste of time sitting in traffic. I'm glad Mia's growing up and can look after herself if I'm late home. And her Dad's just round the corner. In fact on her way home. And he's usually back by 5 pm.

• *What's your new house like?*

It's on Sebert Road, about halfway down, just past the infant school. I like the space. Don't know how I'm going to cope with the garden unless I grass the lot and mow it once a month. Lots of space – three bedrooms upstairs. One I use as my office. Big kitchen, sitting room on the ground floor. It's not badly decorated, in fact we'll have to live with it as I haven't the energy to start decorating and I don't really want anyone in when I'm not there.

- *What about employing Jack to do it?*

That's possible, I suppose. But you do have to be careful. Getting him too close again. And we do argue so much. But I could trust him to decorate and not steal anything. The trouble is if anything went wrong there'd be another level of resentment. I'll think about it. I'm sick of moving. And I hope this is it for some time. It's just the school. I have to get it into shape. If I can.

- *How's your love life?*

What love life? Not totally true. I went on a dating website. Looking for someone local. I was a bit unprepared for the rush. I suppose I'm a bit of a catch. House owner, good salary, still got my figure and, they tell me, my looks. There's a Polish man I quite like the look of. He's very chatty, quite amusing and only lives round the corner. He's asked me out. And I'm thinking, have I got the energy for this? Isn't school as much as I can cope with? And yet – I would like someone. I feel so lonely. Someone easy and there. He seems to have his own money. A property developer he called himself. I'm not quite sure what that is. Does he own property or buy it for other people? He's invited me out for dinner and I'm wondering what to say.

EXERCISE 7

Invent a family, with two parents and three grown up siblings. Give them names. The parents own a restaurant and call a meeting as they want to retire. What are the siblings' attitudes to the retirement, who sides with whom?

My Answer

The family are Greek Cypriots, the parents are planning to go back to Cyprus. They want to sell the restaurant and buy a guest house by the sea. I looked up Greek names on Google. The family are:

Parents, in their 60s, both work in the restaurant, mother as chef and father as head waiter

- Ezio Spyridon, the father
- Agnes Spyridon, the mother

Their Children

- George, son, aged 32

- Kriso, son, 29

- Healani, daughter, 30

George works in the restaurant. He's a good cook, and has worked as a waiter too. He doesn't want his parents to sell the restaurant as he wants to take over. He's worked in it for 14 years and feels he deserves to take it over for all the work he's put in.

Healani sides with George. She is an accountant. She thinks the restaurant could do better and has ideas to improve it. Having done so, they could then borrow money and get a second restaurant going. She thinks their parents have been too complacent. She is always arguing with Kriso, her younger brother, from when they were kids.

Kriso wants his parents to sell the restaurant and go to Cyprus. Not so much for himself but to thwart George and Healani. He worked in the restaurant for a couple of years and hated it. He is now a painter and decorator, and feels Healani, especially, looks down on him.

The meeting will be a family row, all the resentments coming out. There could be a murder yet.

EXERCISE 8

Write a single visual aspect for each of two characters. Make it striking.

My Answer

- He was continually picking his nose with his little finger. And when no one was looking, chewing the snot. It was the habit of a lonely person. He didn't know he was doing it, as he had been doing it so long.

- She was tattooed everywhere, all the way up her arms, round her neck, climbing onto her cheeks and forehead.

EXERCISE 9

Reread the dialogue in this chapter between Jack and Liz. Imagine you are in the park going for a stroll. It is autumn, leaves falling.

Write in first person as yourself. Have a chat with Jack about the work he is doing, rebuilding the wall. Then go to the greenhouse and have a chat with Liz. Just a few minutes with them; they are working, you're not.

My Answer

Leaves were blowing along the drive as I
came through the gates. Ahead I could see
a man in overalls working. He was
youngish, with curly hair, and was
knocking bricks out of the wall along the
bowling green. It had a bulge in it and
clusters of bricks were lying on the
grass behind it. I'd only been in the
park two days ago, and the wall had been
OK then. Something had hit it.

'What's been going on here?' I said as
I approached. 'The damage.'

'A tractor hit it.' He smiled at me,
holding a club hammer and chisel and
wearing safety goggles.

'How on earth can a tractor hit that?'
I exclaimed, stretching my arms along the
damage. 'He must've been drunk.'

'Got it in one,' said the builder. 'Out
drinking over lunch. Came back two sheets
to the wind. And bish, bang, wallop. Hit
the wall. Damaged the tractor. And got
the sack.'

'Not surprised,' I said, looking over
the wall. 'He won't get another job.'

'Not if he asks for a reference,' said
the builder. 'Stand back.'

I did so, as he knocked two bricks out
of the wall with the club hammer. Cement
chippings flew. I figured I'd better
leave him. He had work to do, if I
didn't.

'Good building,' I said.

'I'll do my best,' he said.

And I left him. Seems a nice chap. I
quite envied him, working in the park,

all the trees and sky while I'm stuck in an office. Then again, not so pleasant mid winter or on a rainy day.

I thought why not go to the greenhouse. Warm in there. There's that woman there, Liz. Knows her stuff.

I strolled past the yard. There was no one in there. All out working. There was a big leaf sucker on the lawn. So noisy, I wouldn't like to work on that all day. I walked by the high wall with the Virginia creeper, bulging red as if in pain. We have some on our house wall at home. I always feel it has been pricked with pins.

I opened the greenhouse door and the heat hit me in a whoosh. The air was thick and humid. It was like coming out of one dimension into another.

There was Liz in a t-shirt and jeans, a red scarf tied round her hair. She was watering the greenery in the staging. I had no idea what most of it was. Lush, very green.

'It's like the rain forest in here,' I said.

'A little too cultivated,' she said. 'And no birds or snakes.'

'You could have a recording,' I said. 'Chimps howling and parrots screeching.'

'That would work better for the big glass house at Kew,' she said. 'This is rather small for a jungle.'

I had to agree.

'Do you get colds?' I said, not quite sure where the thought came from. 'Coming from outside to this heat.'

'When I get school parties, and someone's got the sniffles...' she said, continuing to water with her large can. 'Sometimes I pick it up. Bugs love this atmosphere. Warm and moist. An occupational hazard.'

'Like the office where I work,' I said. 'One person gets a cold. Next day we've all got it. What's that plant?'

I had spotted a large plant in flower. Almost like a bird with a beak.

'That's Strelitza reginae,' she said. 'Or bird of paradise.'

'Quite majestic,' I said, walking over to it.

'It is rather,' she said. 'Though they can get a bit fussy.' She hesitated a second and then added, 'I like working in the greenhouse, but I prefer my plants to be wild.'

'I saw you out drawing the other day.'

She smiled. Her face was freckled, hair red. 'You caught me at it,' she said. 'I love autumn days. All the reds and browns, the fruits and mushrooms.' She shook her watering can. 'Must fill up.'

And she went to the far end of the greenhouse. I stayed a few more minutes, the heat though was getting at me, prickling my neck. I was overdressed for a heated greenhouse. And I left.

EXERCISE 10

Write a piece in the first person. Say
500 words. Now change this to third
person, add a few authorial thoughts.

My Answer

I've taken the beginning of *Hard Cash* (in Chapter 11) and
changed it from 1st person to 3rd.

Warby had asked him to write it. He'd
said that Shorty was the one who was good
at that sort of thing and he was sick of
people saying things that just weren't
true. As for Shorty himself - he just
wants to get it out. There was a lot of
talk anyway - so they might as well hear
how it was rather than a load of lies.
Well, one of them had to put them right.
  Shorty was trying to work out where to
begin. If he was going to write it all
down, how much does a reader want to
know. Should there be description of
houses and things? It was harder than he
thought, telling a long story. Nor was it
the sort of tale he'd choose to write.

Stuff description; it would bore any reader as much reading it as would bore him writing it.

He liked adventure; especially space stories - strange planets and far galaxies. He liked a tale to move so that you can't put it down, you want to know so badly what happens next.

None of this description and stuff. So jump in to where it began. Get on with it. Other bits can wait till they are needed. If they are at all. There was this derelict building on Chrisp Street. It wasn't the only derelict building - there were half a dozen of them in a row, all tinned up. Doors, windows - no glass, just corrugated iron. The yards were full of rubbish. Old armchairs, black bags full of rotting rubbish, mattresses, a broken washing machine. You know the sort of stuff that gets dumped.

He'd managed some description hardly being aware he was doing it. Maybe he could do it, he thought.

He mustn't interrupt himself. And press on.

This house had the corrugated iron over the door loose. Not very loose, a bit loose. And then Warby encouraged it. He was never one to hold back and he can be a bit silly. Like when he made faces at those big kids and got himself beat up. Dancing up and down, 'Can't catch me'. Well they could alright and they did alright. You'd think maybe he would learn but Shorty didn't think he ever would.

EXERCISE 11

You are going to write a series of
crime novels with the same main
character and set in your area. Come up
with titles that connect in some way
for the first six novels.

My Answer

My first crime book for adults was a novella entitled *Murder at Any Price*. It's a thriller with Jim Price on the run having been set up for murder. For this exercise, my thinking is: suppose I made Jim a detective, an amateur I think. How about 'Price' in the first six titles:

- *Murder at Any Price*
- *The Price is Right*
- *No Fixed Price*
- *Don't Pay the Price*
- *Everyone has a Price*
- *The Price She Wanted*

It is intriguing with just the titles to imagine what those books might be about. *The Price is Right*, I think someone is out to kill him. *No Fixed Price*, someone is trying to buy him off. *The Price She Wanted* – that could be blackmail and romance.

EXERCISE 12

Two detectives are questioning a suspect. The suspect has been held for questioning but not yet charged. The detectives believe the suspect did it. The suspect has a lawyer present.

Begin with introductions. What are the detective ranks? Write 500 words from one of the detectives' point of view as the interview proceeds. The detectives have a good item of evidence. Hold it back, but use it. How will the suspect react?

To do this exercise I wrote myself the following notes:

DS Fayyad Kamani
DC Hayley Amis
The Suspect: Bertram Poll (objects to being called Bertram, says 'Bert')

The Lawyer: Max Stuart

The interview room: bare apart from the table and chairs. A video camera high up in the corner. Fayyad has the remote for it.

Fayyad in a smart suit, Hayley in one too, so is Max Stuart the lawyer, Bertram Poll is in a T-shirt with "West Ham for the Cup" motif, and jeans. Short cropped hair, tattooed arms, one a twisted serpent going from round his arm from wrist to shoulder, the other thorns and roses almost hiding a castle.

Bert 'No comments' to begin with. Then Fayyad annoys him and Bert says, 'Don't they have any white guys in this station?'

The evidence is a knife with Bert's fingerprints on. There is another suspect, Tom Brady, also being questioned. There is a knock on the door. It is a trick they have come up with. Hayley goes out for a minute. Comes back and says, Tom says you did it, Bert.

[I didn't use all of the plan before getting to 500 words.]

My Answer

'For the record,' said Kamani, 'present for this interview are myself, Detective Sergeant Fayyad Kamani, Detective Constable Hayley Amis, lawyer Max Stuart and Bertram Poll.'

'Bert,' said the burly man opposite him, by the side of his lawyer. 'Only my mother calls me Bertram.'

'I will refer to you as Bert then,' said Kamani. He glanced down at his notes. 'You killed Acme Lahar, Mr Poll.'

'Bert.' He was almost smirking, bare-armed in a T shirt saying West Ham for the Cup. Both arms were fully tattooed. One with a serpent going round the arm from wrist to shoulder, the other had thorns and roses almost hiding a castle.

'You killed Acme Lahar, Bert, didn't you?'

'Who?'

'This man.' Fayyad presented a photograph of a black man in his 30s.

'Never seen him before.'

'Then how come there are nine messages from him on your phone?'

'Seen, seen,' hissed Bert. 'Do you know the word? Seen.' He looked about him nonchalantly. 'Ain't they got any white guys in this station?'

'There's you, Mr Poll, and your lawyer,' said Fayyad. 'And your accomplice Tom Brady.'

'At detective grade, I mean. Those who have English as their mother tongue.'

Max Stuart put a hand on his shoulder, and said quietly. 'This won't help you, Bert.'

Bert threw his hand off roughly and scowled. 'Nothing I do is going to help. This Paki has got me lined up for it. Am I right?'

'We think this was a racist crime,' said Fayyad. 'And you are certainly a racist, Bert.'

'Yeh, I admit it. What of it?'

Fayyad slipped another photo from his papers.

'Is this your knife?' he said.

Bert looked at the photo. Turned it around. He shrugged.

'No comment.'

'Would you tell us why it has your fingerprint on it?'

'No comment.' He turned to his lawyer. 'Can I insist on being questioned by a white cop?'

'No, you can't,' said Stuart.

'I don't know what this country is coming to. What's happened to the Magna Carta? An Englishman's right to be tried by his peers.'

Hayley nudged Kamani. He nodded.

'You were in communication with Acme Lahar,' she said. 'We have your fingerprint on the knife that killed him, Bertram...'

'What is it with you cops? Bert! Bert! Bert! I have a right to be called by my preferred name. Only my mum calls me Bertram.' He leaned forward over the table. 'You my Mum?'

'Difficult,' she said. 'I'm two years younger than you, Mr Poll.'

'And you have a Paki for a partner.'

'This is all on record, Mr Poll,' said Fayyad. 'If it's used in court, your attitude and language won't be to your advantage.'

'Might I have a private word with my client, DS Kamani?'

'I'm sure he needs one.' Fayyad took up the remote. 'Interview terminated while the suspect talks to his lawyer.'

He clicked the remote and stood up, Hayley stood too.

'We'll leave for ten minutes.'

The two detectives walked to the door.

'Get us a cuppa, will you, darling.' Bert winked at Hayley.

Thank you!

I am grateful to every reader who finishes one of my books. There are plenty of things you could have been doing, other than reading this book. So, thank you for your time. If you liked *Writing A Crime Novel*, here's what you can do next:

I'd appreciate a review on Amazon. In that way, you can help me tell other readers about my books. Without reviews authors get few sales. So I'd be grateful for your review to help this book be better known.

You can get a **FREE** ebook of *Jack of Spades* if you visit my website and sign up for my readers' list.

You may give it to a friend if you wish. When you sign up for my readers' list you will receive my regular newsletter. This will give you news about me, what I'm reading, and tell you about my future books, PLUS a variety of giveaways.

DerekSmithWriter.com

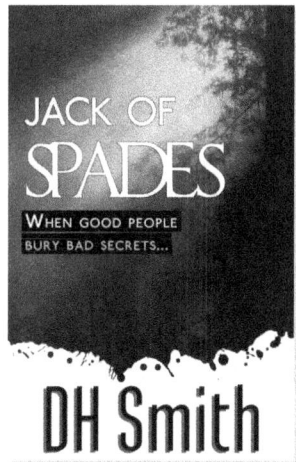

JACK OF
SPADES

WHEN GOOD PEOPLE
BURY BAD SECRETS...

DH Smith

Crime Novels by DH Smith

Jack Bell

These are all standalone novels and can be read in any order. They are:

- *Jack of All Trades*
- *Jack of Spades*
- *Jack o'Lantern*
- *Jack By The Hedge*
- *Jack In The Box*
- *Jack On The Tower*
- *Jack Recalled*
- *Jack At Death's Door*
- *Jack At The Gate*

Some Amazon reviews

Well written from the first page to the last page. I have definitely found a new author

The story grabs you, sucks you in, and leaves you guessing, providing juicy dialogue and laugh-out-loud moments along the way

A different type of mystery where the main personality is not a professional crime solver, but a builder/carpenter with his own personal issues

Other Books

Murder at Any Price

Books by Derek Smith

All my other books are written under the name Derek Smith.

Fantasy

Hell's Chimney
The Prince's Shadow

Other

Strikers of Hanbury Street (short stories)
Catching Up (poetry)

Young Adult Novels

Hard Cash
Half a Bike
Fast Food
Frances Fairweather Demon Striker!

Children's Novels

The Good Wolf
Feather Brains
Baker's Boy

For Younger Children

The Magical World of Lucy-Anne
Lucy-Anne's Changing Ways
Jack's Bus

About the Author

I live in Forest Gate in the East End of London. In my working life, I have been a plastics chemist, a gardener and a
stage manager before becoming a professional writer. I
began with plays, working with several theatre companies,
and had a few plays on radio and TV, as well as on the stage.

In the early 80s I became involved in running a co-operat-
ive bookshop and vegetarian café in Stratford, where I
learned to cook, and had my first go at writing a novel. The
first was a mess, and, after too many rewrites, binned. The
transition from drama to novels took me a couple of years
to get to grips with.

My first success was a young adult novel, *Hard Cash*, published by Faber. Buoyed up by this, I stuck with children's
work, did school visits, and made a hand to mouth living as
a full time author, topped up with some evening class work
in creative writing at City University and the Mary Ward
Centre in Holborn. A few adult fiction titles appeared from
time to time, between the children's list, and I have since
been working more in that direction with my *Jack of All
Trades* series.

www.DerekSmithWriter.com

The book you've been reading was designed by Lia at

Contact lia@freeyourwords.com for a quote

9 781909 804364